TRAVELS WITH A WILDLIFE ARTIST

For our children Sophie and Ben
and for the many friends met and made
in Greece

Manx shearwaters skimming over the
waves near an uninhabited island in the
Cyclades.

TRAVELS WITH A WILDLIFE ARTIST

THE LIVING LANDSCAPE OF GREECE

PETER & SUSAN BARRETT

Foreword by Gerald Durrell

COLUMBUS BOOKS
LONDON

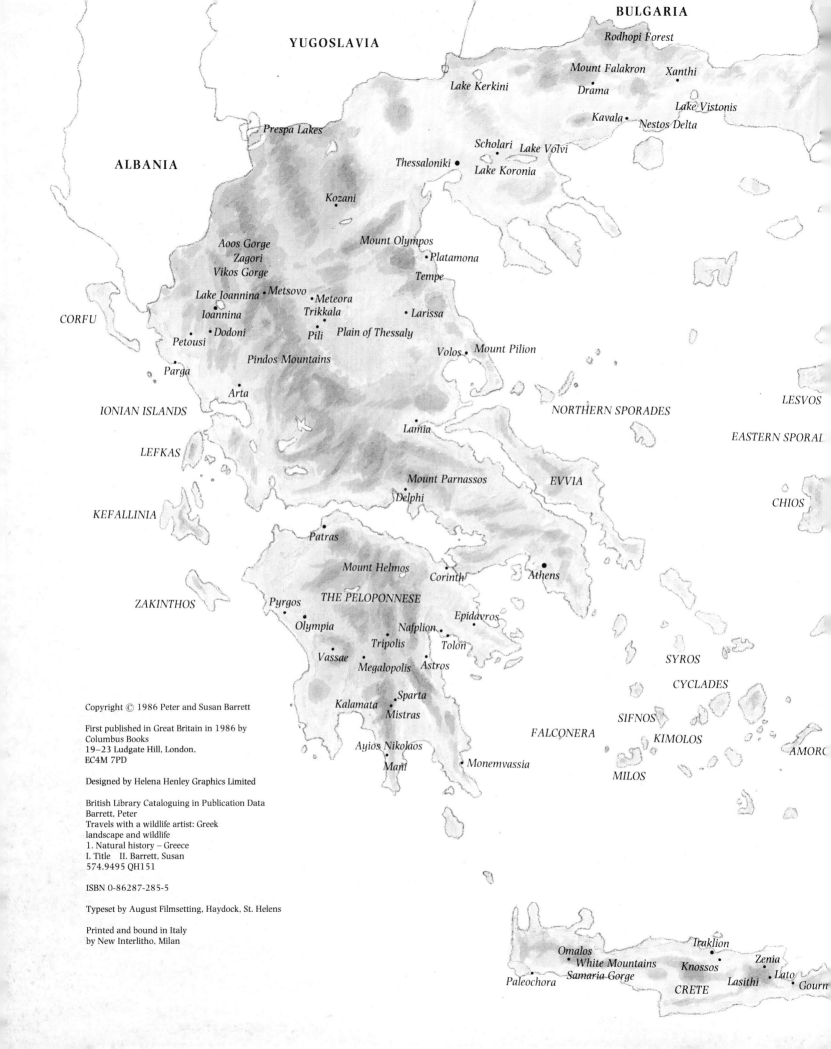

YUGOSLAVIA

BULGARIA

Rodhopi Forest

Lake Kerkini

Mount Falakron · Xanthi
· Drama

Kavala · Nestos Delta · Lake Vistonis

Prespa Lakes

ALBANIA

Scholari · Lake Volvi
Thessaloniki · Lake Koronia

Kozani

Aoos Gorge
Zagori
Vikos Gorge

Mount Olympos
· Platamona
Tempe

Lake Ioannina · Metsovo
· Meteora
Ioannina · Trikkala · Larissa
· Dodoni · Pili Plain of Thessaly
Petousi Pindos Mountains Volos · Mount Pilion

CORFU

Parga

Arta

IONIAN ISLANDS

Lamia

NORTHERN SPORADES

LESVOS

LEFKAS

EASTERN SPORAI

Mount Parnassos
Delphi

EVVIA

CHIOS

KEFALLINIA

Patras

Mount Helmos
Corinth · Athens

THE PELOPONNESE

ZAKINTHOS

Pyrgos

Epidavros

Olympia
Tripolis · Nafplion
Vassae · Tolon
Megalopolis Astros

SYROS

CYCLADES

Kalamata · Sparta
Mistras

SIFNOS
FALCONERA KIMOLOS

AMOR(

Ayios Nikolaos
Mani · Monemvassia

MILOS

Copyright © 1986 Peter and Susan Barrett

First published in Great Britain in 1986 by
Columbus Books
19–23 Ludgate Hill, London,
EC4M 7PD

Designed by Helena Henley Graphics Limited

British Library Cataloguing in Publication Data
Barrett, Peter
Travels with a wildlife artist: Greek
landscape and wildlife
1. Natural history – Greece
I. Title   II. Barrett, Susan
574.9495 QH151

ISBN 0-86287-285-5

Typeset by August Filmsetting, Haydock, St. Helens

Printed and bound in Italy
by New Interlitho, Milan

Omalos · Traklion
· White Mountains Knossos · Zenia
Samaria Gorge · Lasithi · Lato
Paleochora CRETE Gourn

TURKEY

TURKEY

AMOS

TMOS

LIPSI

LEROS

EVITHA

KALIMNOS

DODECANESE

RHODES

CONTENTS

Foreword by Gerald Durrell 6

An ending and a beginning   7

Foreword

This is a beautifully written and illustrated book, one that will be enormously evocative to those who know Greece and to those who don't it will fill them with a yearning to go there instantly.

It is rare that you get a married couple who complement each other as well as Susan and Peter Barrett do, for her magical prose complements his delicate and lovely pictures so well and his pictures add a new dimension to the prose.

I read it on one of those grey, freezing, spring days with flurries of rain hitting the windows like buckshot and I was immediately transported back to Greece, all the scents and sounds and colours trapped between the covers of the book, giving me a much-needed vacation on a day that even a snowdrop would have considered inclement.

It is obvious that the author and artist not only have a deep love for Greece but for the Greeks themselves and this important element comes through very forcefully in the book. It is rare to read a work like this, where nothing seems to escape the author's eye, whether it is a ruined temple, a rubbish tip, goats having a sand bath or a butterfly flirting with a shirt. It is the sort of book that you wish you had written yourself.

This is a volume that must be in the luggage of every traveller to what is one of the most enchanting countries in the world.

Gerald Durrell.

AN ENDING AND A BEGINNING

Over the harbour of Igoumenitsa lightning tears away strips of black night sky, and an anchored ship, a sliver of sea and the low outlines of islets are briefly visible in a pinkish monotone, like after-images on a closed eyelid. These are the last images of Greece as we leave in late October; this is the last of the journeys working on this book. Writing now on the ferry bound for Italy, it's hard to concentrate. A German passenger, who was Military Attaché at the embassy in the early 'seventies has much of interest to say. Over the shuddering of the engines, there are murmurings in Italian, American, English, French, German and Greek. Each language has its own cadence and the Greek, now in a minority, exerts a powerful nostalgia. With Greek music in the background, it is easy to feel maudlin at departure. This is a country of constant arrivals and departures; a welter of small communities, villages and islands where there is a continual coming and going. All the special phrases that are exchanged on these occasions are like minute hooks. There can be few visitors to Greece who have never wished to return. The hooks are there, invisible and tenacious and yes, though we may be leaving now, we will be back.

We first arrived in 1962 and for the next ten years made our life here, with only the occasional short absence. During the last three years we have travelled round Greece, looking and listening and learning, and recording what we have seen and heard and learnt. This spring we met Byron Antipas of the Hellenic Society for the Protection of Nature, who overflowed with information about specialists, scientists and studies. It made us realize how much there is to learn about wildlife in Greece, how great a need there is for education and how impossible it is to give more than a hint of this in one book. Yet books can be persuasive. The manageress of an Athens hotel was puzzled by requests from all over the world for one particular room; its praises, she learnt, had been sung in a recent guide book. A young American, whom we met last week in Dodoni and gave a lift to Ioannina, was looking for the Greece of such writers as Kevin Andrews and Patrick Leigh Fermor. Were it not for their books, he might not have been in Greece at all. It is now 23 October. In five days' time, Greece will be celebrating the anniversary of the day in 1940 when Metaxas the Prime Minister said 'No' to the Italians. Instead of walking over the Albanian frontier to occupy Greece as they expected, the Italians found themselves fighting a long winter battle. The Military Attaché is telling me that he was in Ioannina on that day, part of the German garrison. He offers me a biscuit made in Israel. The packet lies on the table beside a book: *Pausanias' Guide to Greece*, written in the 2nd Century AD.

The juxtaposition of time, place, people and events is as intriguing as the fragments of a kaleidoscope. I find myself hoping that the notebooks and sketches of the last three years can somehow be shaken like a kaleidoscope so that, however ordinary each piece is, a pattern will emerge. Ours is not a guide book. It is a personal selection of places seen with the eyes of an artist interested in nature and a novelist interested in everything. If it raises curiosity and enthusiasm in its readers, then it will send them to learn more from other, specialist books. If our book turns out to be persuasive, I would like its readers to join the Hellenic Society for the Protection of Nature. And may they have as good a time travelling in Greece as we have had.

SUSAN BARRETT

Igoumenitsa, Brindisi

Crete

Sometimes in winter, in the midst of harsh weather when north-east winds straight from the steppes of Russia cut through the thickest overcoats, there will be a sudden calm, when the sea lies flat as glass and the atmosphere is bright and soft in gentle sun. These are halcyon days – days of the kingfisher. The name has a legendary history.

Alcyone and her husband the King of Trachis had been drowned and turned into kingfishers. As the rough winter gales kept destroying their floating nests, Alcyone's father – the wind god Aeolus – promised to allow them a fortnight's calm every year at the time of the winter solstice. In fact, kingfishers build their nests in banks much later in the year, and 'kingfisher days' come singly and in January. However, Queen Alcyone gave her name to the bird, to the rare calm days of mid-winter, and in other languages to times of peace and happiness.

On such days it is possible to look south from the high land of a Cycladean island and see Mount Ida of Crete breaking the line between sea and sky like a legend's illustration.

Crete, the largest and southernmost island of Greece, lies in a long horizontal only 322 kilometres from the coast of Africa. The peninsulas and islands of Greece seem to point towards it, depending for their safety on the strong high barrier it forms, like a fortress wall. This illusion is strengthened by the way the mountain ranges that run the length of the island lie closer to the southern coast, descending sharply towards the sea and Africa, while the land slopes more gently towards the low northern coast and Greece.

Because of the island's size, isolation and climate, there are more species of wild flowers growing here than anywhere else in Greece, and as many as 155 of these are found nowhere else. In the White Mountains to the west, it is sometimes possible to catch a glimpse of the *agrimi*, the Cretan wild goat, poised momentarily on a high and seemingly inaccessible pinnacle. Rarest sight of all is the magnificent lammergeier vulture. It is thought there may be only 30 or so pairs left in Greece. In the remoter parts of the island, it is possible to see not only the lammergeier but many other species of vulture and birds of prey, in mountainous scenery of spectacular beauty.

In the south west of Crete yellow is a predominant colour in spring. There are the yellows of asphodel, Asphodeline lutea, Jerusalem sage, Phlomis fruticosa, and various kinds of broom. This hillside, inland from Paleochora, is a mass of spiny broom, Calicotome villosa.

Opposite: alpine choughs float in air currents above the Gorge of Samaria. This gigantic split in the earth's surface, the longest true gorge in Europe, runs from a height of 1000 metres in the White Mountains down to sea level at Ayia Roumeli, 18 kilometres away.

Gournia and Lato

A party of foreigners has arrived at Gournia, and gathered on a shallow flight of steps in the Minoan town. They have been handed sheets of paper by their leader, one sheet each. It is a plan of the ruins. They will do this properly.

The terrace is dotted with turban buttercups. Each golden cup trembles above the earth supported by a green thread of a stem, barely visible. They are a defiant sort of flower, single, boldly coloured, growing out of stone. Asphodel are everywhere. They can afford to look lacey and delicate because they are supported so strongly by the candelabra stem growing from the huge hidden bulb. Pale lilac anemones cluster in cracks. A mass of violet-coloured iris, *Gynandriris sisyrinchium*, have unfolded their heads to the sun. Earlier in the day, in the churchyard of Panayia Kera, the irises stood furled shut.

In the far distance a herd of sheep and goats move across a low tawny hill, their bells clamouring.

The position of many ancient sites seems arbitrary. Often they seem simply to have happened on any old hill – not the most imposing in the area, and sometimes not even on top of a hill at all, but down the side of a nondescript slope. Yet when you have arrived and are in the midst of the ruins, then you feel you are somewhere and yes, perhaps it was a good place to build. Gournia is a particularly arbitrary site – why there? By contrast, Lato makes sense straight away. The two peaks command immense distances, the saddle between the two is sheltered, and below the saddle, held suspended like a hammock, lies a deep enclosed green and fertile valley, totally hidden and protected.

The sculptural shapes of the cypress, Cupressus sempervirens, *frame the fourteenth-century church of Panayia Kera at Kritsa. Here the frescoes are among the finest and best preserved in Crete. In April the forecourt is studded with* Gynandriris sisyrinchium, *an iris with bright blue flowers that unfurl only after midday.*

An old man with his sheep points the way to Lato. He chats about his rheumatism, induced by years of damp cave dwelling as a partisan in the war. Meanwhile his herd of sheep, looking like whippets that have accidentally crawled under shaggy rugs, seize the chance to spread in all directions. An angry daughter, swearing and cursing her father as much as the sheep, appears between the wild pear trees. She gathers the animals together and leads them to graze on a thinly green terrace, turning her head to shout rebukes at the idly chatting man. He is in no hurry to move away. He leans on his crook, and hitches his half-hung coat further up his shoulder. He talks of living in the mountain caves, the raids the partisans carried out, and the reprisals in the villages afterwards. In one particular village, he says, 130 were killed.

A hoopoe flies fast and low through the olive groves, where the track leaves the fertile plain and winds up the rough hillside. Griffon vultures wheel in the sky. At the top lies Lato, a high warm place strung between two peaks. Stone walls appear in rich undergrowth. Boulders lie amid starry white camomile, buttercup, and the clumped blades of sea squill that will soon wither in the hot sun to flower in the autumn rains. Spring asphodel stands filtering the sun through its spires of pale lilac pink. Under a carob grows a group of poisonous-looking plants with thick stems daubed with cream brushmarks: dragon arum, not yet in flower. Scarce swallowtails flicker in great numbers, belying their name. Delicate stems of thin rushes waver on the rim of a deep green bowl. The hillsides descend to this bowl of a valley in steep terraces of olive, carob, flowering almond and prickly kermes oak. Among the trees, chiff-chaffs, willow warblers and goldfinches sing.

From the peaks it is possible to see the surrounding land laid out far below, chequered fertile plains stretching away to distant mountains. To the north, barely visible above a swoop of sage-coloured hills, the white cube-sugar hump of Ayios Nikolaos marks the thin blue line of sea.

This is a tranquil place, close to the sky, isolated from the life below, and silent save for the song of the birds and the steady underlying buzz of insects in the undergrowth.

Dracunculus vulgaris, *the dragon arum, grows to a metre high from April to June, usually on waste ground. The flower is a deep brownish-purple spathe, but in Crete a white-flowered form is sometimes found.*

By a threshing floor among carob, olive and wild pear trees a hoopoe raises its black-tipped crest. These birds are often seen flying fast and low through olive groves. Their name echoes their low, hooting call.

11

Chameleons are slow-moving lizards of Africa and southern Asia, but one species has found its way to two areas of Europe: southern Spain and Crete. This is the Mediterranean chameleon. With prehensile tail and feet adapted to curling round twigs and branches, it can be found in bushes and trees in dry areas. Its ability to adopt the colour of its background is its best-known feature. Normally green, it can turn a blotchy white, grey or brown. When disturbed it becomes very dark and inflates itself with air to almost twice its normal size.

A deep ravine divides a high spur of Mount Dikti from a steep, terraced hillside where almond, apple and wild pear trees are wreathed in blossom.

Above Zenia

The olive trees this year have been burnt by heavy snow and frost. They stand blackened on the terraces, and are now being heavily pruned. A 73-year-old man, working a few terraces below, brings glasses, a bottle of *tsikoudhia* and a handful of almonds. These terraces, he says, were thick with almonds, but some years ago the trees were struck by a disease which withered them. Even specialists with various insecticides could not solve the problem. The man lists his complaints. He is melancholy, not without cause.

'Once there were so many of us working these terraces. Now no one wants to work. The young have only a few interests...' (he counts them on his fingers) '...football, cigarettes, theatres, cinemas and women.' It is a little hard, looking at the great expanse of mountainous landscape, to imagine where these interests might be found. 'They don't want to work to get their bread. I've had ten operations. I'm stronger now, but...' Meanwhile, as he talks and drinks, his wife hacks away at the earth further down the steep hillside. The hoe chunks and rings as it sinks in the red earth and hits a stone. The earth is the colour of dried blood. A grey stone when split reveals terracotta. A road cut in a hillside is a jagged scar, the revealed colour a wound that may never heal. The same colour covers the reconstructed pillars of the palace of Knossos, and the reconstruction influences the decoration of new building today: bulls'-horn patterns, and terracotta pillars.

Higher up the hillside another hoe hacks the earth, and the voices of a woman and children echo in the blue space. A tiny rushing stream hurtles down a crease in the mountainside. Peter draws the wild almond and pear blossom. The colours are vivid in the sun and against the sky. There is grass on the terraces, and in the grass, the spiked blades of emerging gladioli. There are anemones, in shades of lilac, mauve and purple; huge, glistening yellow celandine; and a flower which looks like a cross between an iris and an orchid. Three sprays of creamy green arch out from the stem and end in a globule of purple. This is snake's-head iris, *Hermodactylus tuberosus*. Steeply this intense colour under the hot sun disappears down to an unseen depth before the mountains opposite. The greyish pink and sage colours of its sheer creased slopes of scree and scrub are pale in the distance, and disappear finally in a remote and personal wreath of cloud. Little pockets of snow cling in a few crevices. Another country.

The old man talks of his two sons, both teachers at the primary schools of Ayios Nikolaos and Kritsa. One of his daughters-in-law has a hotel and apartments. Very soon, he says, Greece will be ruined: there will be no one to work the terraces.

Yet higher up the hillside a young man has joined the woman and children. He has brought a rotavator. He starts to work on a series of terraces, rebuilt with neat and substantial retaining walls. His van is parked on the newly-made track that winds up the hill from the road below. The track continues to a spring, the source of the stream that tumbles past the old man and his *tsikoudhia*.

Later, the rotavator is put back in the van, and silence returns. The old man and his wife start work on another terrace: he, with a team of oxen ploughing, she hacking away at the ridges between the furrows.

FLOWERS OF THE SPRING
Greece has at least 6,000 species of flora, many of them found nowhere else. Crete alone has 155 endemic species and there is no better place to see spring flowers.

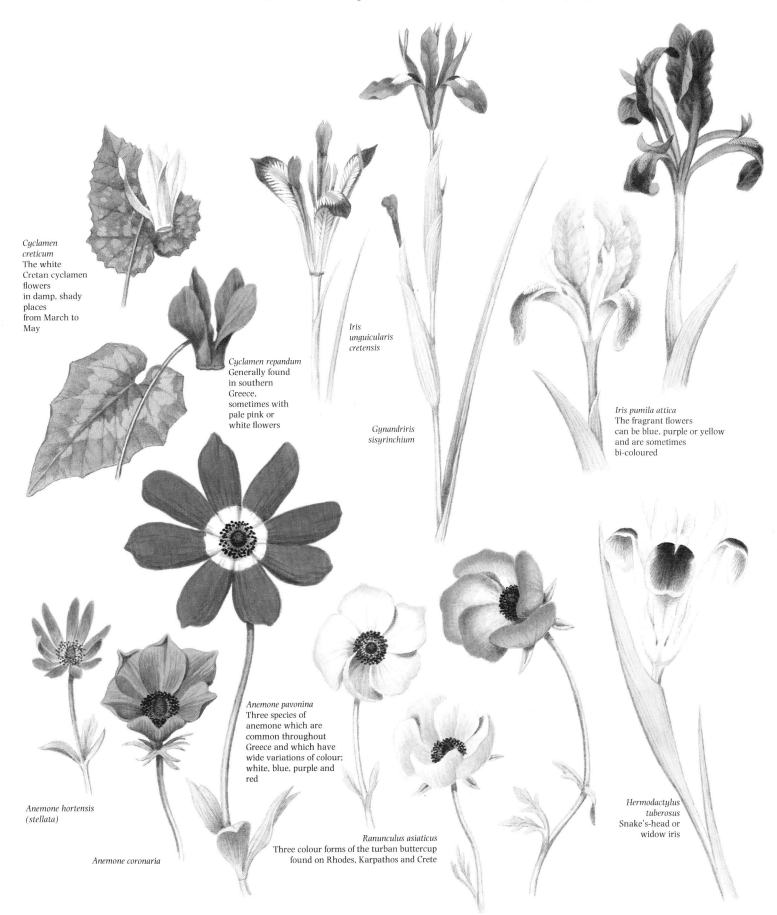

Cyclamen creticum
The white Cretan cyclamen flowers in damp, shady places from March to May

Cyclamen repandum
Generally found in southern Greece, sometimes with pale pink or white flowers

Iris unguicularis cretensis

Gynandriris sisyrinchium

Iris pumila attica
The fragrant flowers can be blue, purple or yellow and are sometimes bi-coloured

Anemone pavonina
Three species of anemone which are common throughout Greece and which have wide variations of colour; white, blue, purple and red

Anemone hortensis (stellata)

Anemone coronaria

Ranunculus asiaticus
Three colour forms of the turban buttercup found on Rhodes, Karpathos and Crete

Hermodactylus tuberosus
Snake's-head or widow iris

On the road to Lasithi

In the valleys the leaves are out, but higher up the slopes almond, peach and pear are still in blossom. Broad beans are planted in tubs by houses, and in small patches in olive groves. There are great drifts of camomile and everywhere the pretty yellow buttercup. This is Bermuda buttercup, or Cape sorrel, which was brought here in the eighteenth century from the Cape of Good Hope. It spreads rapidly by forming bulbils on the surface of the soil and has become a serious weed in orange and olive groves and orchards.

A wild flower is said to have become a weed when it has spread in great numbers and is useless to humans. In fact wild flowers are only safe from being called weeds, and subsequently sprayed away, when they flower in places where people cannot cultivate. Fortunately for many wild flowers, and for the whole interdependent circle of nature of which we are part, there are vast expanses of such areas in Greece.

Ancient sites are nowadays protected from grazing and cultivation, and are often fenced. Wild flowers abound, but there is a growing tendency to spray the weeds. The roots of some shrubs and trees, forcing themselves through walls, may certainly in time cause a ruin to disintegrate completely. Briefly flowering annuals and bulbs can do no harm, and add immensely to the haunting atmosphere of ruined palaces and towns. Somehow, nature adds humanity. Iris and crocuses and lilies, painted with such sensitivity on Minoan vases and frescoes, grow today where the Minoans lived. A fig tree, self-seeded, growing through stones against a single column, links us with the past. A mat of bell-flowered campanula spilling from a crack, the spires of asphodel on ancient pavements, the scarlet anemone, white Star of Bethlehem, the simple daisies and speedwell, and the insects, butterflies, and birds which the flowers and shrubs attract, are all an inherent part of the atmosphere. At Knossos, speckled wood butterflies dance among the almond blossom. The air is heavy with the sweet smell of honey and resin. In Gournia, the pavements are strewn with the varying pinks and mauves of anemones, the deep golden *Ranunculus asiaticus*, and the bright white stars of dwarf ornithogalum. *Orchis italica* marches the terraces of Phaistos. Ayia Triadha harbours an orchid endemic to Crete: *Ophrys cretica*, a whitish orchid with strong deep mauve markings. On the peaks of Lato, where the stones lie deep in the undergrowth which gives the site so much of its magic, grows a campanula found only in Crete, *Petromarula pinnata*, with a stem that can be a metre high. Banish these, and the ancient ruins could lose their power to attract all but a few devoted historians.

A speckled wood butterfly spreads its pale orange and brown wings on almond blossom by the Minoan palace at Knossos. The speckled wood, Pararge aegeria, *is one of the first butterflies to emerge in the spring. There are many almond trees throughout Greece, both wild and cultivated.*

The artists of ancient Minoan times painted natural forms with grace and delicacy. Here Pancratium maritimum, *the lily of the sea or sea daffodil, and* Lilium candidum, *the Madonna lily, are portrayed on wall paintings.*

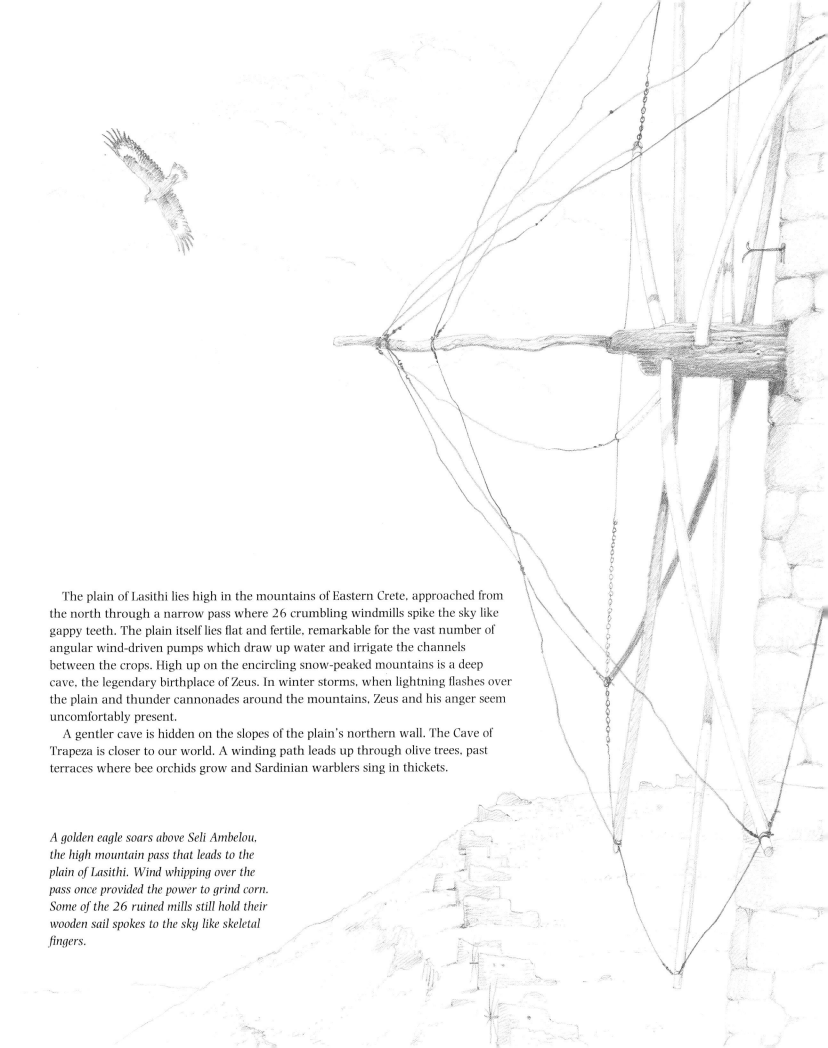

The plain of Lasithi lies high in the mountains of Eastern Crete, approached from the north through a narrow pass where 26 crumbling windmills spike the sky like gappy teeth. The plain itself lies flat and fertile, remarkable for the vast number of angular wind-driven pumps which draw up water and irrigate the channels between the crops. High up on the encircling snow-peaked mountains is a deep cave, the legendary birthplace of Zeus. In winter storms, when lightning flashes over the plain and thunder cannonades around the mountains, Zeus and his anger seem uncomfortably present.

A gentler cave is hidden on the slopes of the plain's northern wall. The Cave of Trapeza is closer to our world. A winding path leads up through olive trees, past terraces where bee orchids grow and Sardinian warblers sing in thickets.

A golden eagle soars above Seli Ambelou, the high mountain pass that leads to the plain of Lasithi. Wind whipping over the pass once provided the power to grind corn. Some of the 26 ruined mills still hold their wooden sail spokes to the sky like skeletal fingers.

THE ORCHIDS OF GREECE
Orchids flower throughout Greece from February to July, depending on altitude and area. Crete has several endemic and increasingly rare orchids.

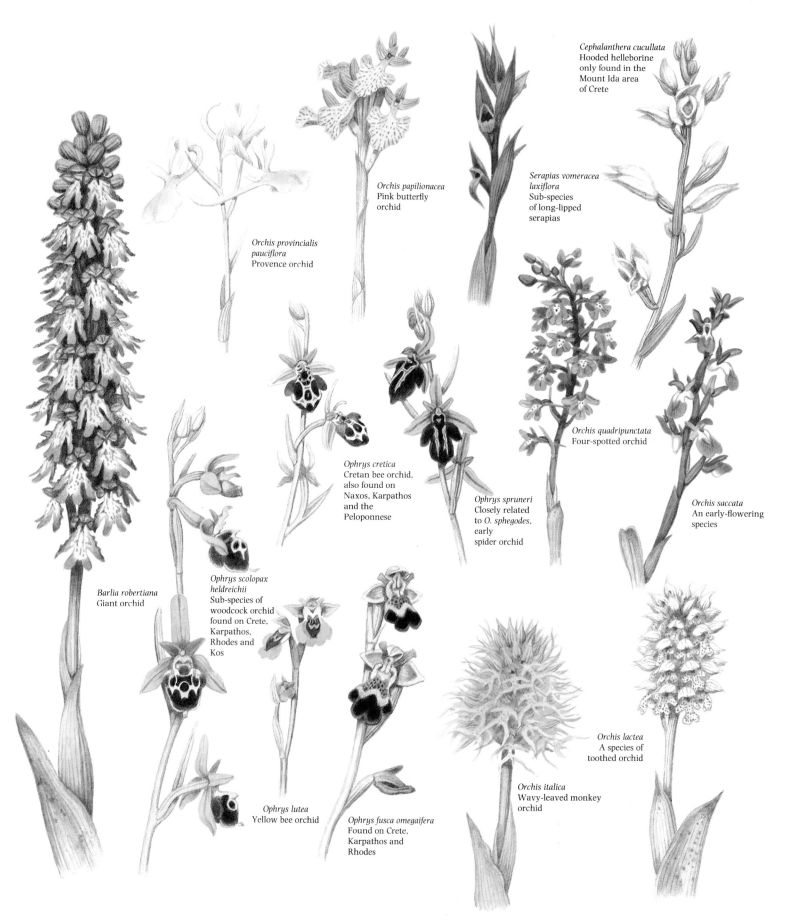

Cephalanthera cucullata
Hooded helleborine
only found in the
Mount Ida area
of Crete

Orchis papilionacea
Pink butterfly
orchid

*Serapias vomeracea
laxiflora*
Sub-species
of long-lipped
serapias

*Orchis provincialis
pauciflora*
Provence orchid

Orchis quadripunctata
Four-spotted orchid

Ophrys cretica
Cretan bee orchid,
also found on
Naxos, Karpathos
and the
Peloponnese

Ophrys spruneri
Closely related
to *O. sphegodes*,
early
spider orchid

Orchis saccata
An early-flowering
species

Barlia robertiana
Giant orchid

*Ophrys scolopax
heldreichii*
Sub-species of
woodcock orchid
found on Crete,
Karpathos,
Rhodes and
Kos

Orchis lactea
A species of
toothed orchid

Ophrys lutea
Yellow bee orchid

Ophrys fusca omegaifera
Found on Crete,
Karpathos and
Rhodes

Orchis italica
Wavy-leaved monkey
orchid

The White Mountains

Off the north-eastern coast near Ayios Nikolaos lies Kri-Kri island which is a protected reserve for the *agrimi*, the Cretan wild goat. Sensibly, no landing is allowed without official permission, but in summer there are boat trips round the island. This is one answer to the dilemma posed by the frail existence of a rare species which some wish to preserve and admire and others to hunt and kill.

In Europe the only genuinely wild goats still remaining are those protected in a few areas of Greece. Besides Kri-Kri island, there are several other small reserves on tiny Aegean islands, but not all the goats are as pure-bred as those found in the White Mountains of Crete. In the past *agrimi* were a common sight throughout the island. It is not surprising that a history of war, poverty, hunger and upheaval led to heavy hunting, and even though laws were introduced in 1950, poaching continued. In 1955, one notorious poacher boasted that he had killed more than 400 goats during his lifetime. As he was only 46 years old, he was clearly devoted to the work. The goats took refuge in an area which defies the hungriest hunter – the White Mountains.

Here, in a network of ravines and gorges and pinnacles of rock, the remaining *agrimi* are relatively safe. Now designated a national animal and awarded a National Park where hunting, grazing and tree-felling are forbidden, they should be free to roam unmolested within the confines of this park. But the safe area covers only about 20 square kilometres and a new pressure has arisen. So many of us visit this once-wild and beautiful region that the *agrimi* have wisely retreated even deeper into the fastness of the mountains. The area where they can escape from poachers and tourists is shrinking every year.

As the number of visitors increases, and the number of those visitors wanting to see rare species also increases, the number of rare species diminishes. Conservationists wish to keep the *agrimi* apart from domesticated flocks. So do the shepherds, whose land this is. But for the shepherds, the best means is still the gun. For, while the motive of the conservationists is to keep the wild strain pure, that of the shepherd is much more pressing – to protect precious grazing land, his livelihood, from competition.

As with the *agrimi*, so with the wolves and bears of Northern Greece, and with the eagles . . .

*A wild goat pauses for a moment on a high crag in the White Mountains. Greece is the only country in Europe where genuinely wild goats still exist. The Cretan wild goat (*agrimi*), Capra aegagrus cretica, is the ancestor of all domestic goats and this area of Crete is its last remaining natural habitat. There are reserves for the* agrimi *on a few Aegean islands but the goats on these are not of pure stock, having interbred in the past with domestic flocks.*

Omalos and the Gorge of Samaria

The rough road climbs steadily from Kandanos, where a large party from a dark-windowed red coach, strangely called the 'Rollende Hotel', clumps purposefully through the village. Have they perhaps come to see the waterworks constructed by a German group in atonement for the destruction of the village in 1941? Or Ancient Kandanos and the frescoes in the two Byzantine churches which lie among trees and flowers above the village? Old men sit stolidly on café chairs along the pavements and watch the people pass. Their faces are expressionless. So many have come and gone in Crete's long history.

Winter rain has washed away the edges of the mountain road and made the margin between safe travel and the dizzy drop a fraction narrower. A buzzard, wheeling overhead, dives towards the road like a kamikaze pilot; then plummets over the edge and straight down out of sight. Turning attention back to the road induces the sensation of a high-speed lift as its upward rush comes to a halt on a skyscraper's top floor.

A thousand metres up, the road pushes its way through the encircling White Mountains and on to the Plain of Omalos, a moonscape in early April. The flat expanse lies grey and empty. It is not yet time to plough the earth, fertile and moist from the winter snows, and plant the summer crops of vegetables. Old and derelict stone-built huts and byres are dotted around the plain, like quaint beach chalets beside an inland sea. In a far corner of the plain there is a group of ramshackle but recently built houses. All is quiet, shuttered, deserted. But in a week or two, the people who work the fields during the summer months will arrive from the villages where they spend the winter. This too gives the place the air of a resort in the off-season – a Swiss lake, perhaps. In the centre of the plain where a pool, not a lake, reflects the blue sky, a few anemones grow among the reedy grasses. Later, the ground will be blazing with wild flowers. But now the only vivid patches of colour lie just below the snowline: the yellow of crocus and the brilliant sky-blue of scilla.

This is an Alpine habitat, far removed – it seems – from the sea by high and solid mountains. Yet this is not so. The plain is, in fact, closely connected with the harbour of Ayia Roumeli. A gigantic split in the rock on the southern side reveals a gorge which leads like a castle's secret passage to the coast.

The air hangs chill. Wooden-railed steps lead down the cliff face where pines find a tenuous foothold and Alpine choughs float in the abyss, now darkly outlined against the patch of blue trapped between the peaks above, now lost in the black shadows far below.

Though closed from 1 November to the end of April because of the danger of rock falls, it is possible during summer to walk the length of the Gorge of Samaria, at 18 kilometres the longest in Europe. Nowadays, with all the conveniences that tourism brings, with buses one end and boats the other, this is an easy enough walk through spectacular scenery. And there is always the chance reward: a glimpse of an *agrimi* or a lammergeier vulture.

In early spring only vultures give life to the bleak and barren plain of Omalos, which later in the year will glow with wild flowers. The griffon vultures on the left and the Egyptian vultures in the centre are a common sight, but the lammergeiers on the right are increasingly rare. Griffon vultures are often confused with eagles in flight but they can be distinguished by their larger size and shorter tail. Here both immature and adult birds are shown with their different markings.

Paleochora

It is unusual to see these two Cretan endemics growing side by side: Aristolochia cretica, *a member of the family commonly called Dutchman's pipe, and the deep pink tulip* Tulipa saxatilis, *which grows mainly in the west of the island.*

In a grassy meadow by a stream the wild flowers create a picture whichever way you turn. By the striped funnel of Arisarum vulgare, *aptly called friar's cowl,* Ophrys cretica *raises its head above* Ophrys scolopax *and in the foreground* Orchis papilionacea *is shown in its brightest colour form.*

It is twenty years since our last visit to Paleochora. Then two cars bumped their way over the boulders of a track that was more like a dried river-bed than a road. The village, straggling out to sea on a long snout of land, was viewed as paradise by one car-load. Our friends the Burges and their baby remained in Paleochora, the prospect of the awful return journey adding greatly to the village's attraction. It is as charming a straggle as it was then, but now on a larger scale. The harbour, where the snout finally dips into the sea, is like a curling tongue licking up boats. This headland gives the town two profiles. One subsides into the sea in a rocky, scrappy way, and the other faces a grand sweep of fine, clean sand. On this side new buildings sprout as though escaping from the narrow confines of the original long street. American and Australian Greeks have returned to serve Greek specialities to American, Australian, German and French youth. Yes, the baker's wife tells an American family, she too has lived in the States, in New Jersey.

The wooded hillsides above the town are glowing with the golden flowers of spiny broom. An old man with a broad white moustache, a band of fringed cloth round his forehead, Cretan breeches and boots, turns to wave. He and the two grandchildren with him have been gathering *horta*, edible weeds, which they carry in woven bags of purple and red stripes. Five cheerful dogs bound at their heels.

Below the road there is a rushing stream, hidden and overhung with plane trees. Peter sits on the bank and paints the jumbled grey boulders where the water froths white and plentiful. This is a magical place of dappled sunshine and a tracery of oleander and smooth, twisted plane branches, moist yellow-green crinkle-edged leaves just emerging. Butterflies, Cleopatra brimstones and common blues, flicker in the dark ivy festooned over boulders and tree trunks. Cyclamen, bone-china white, hold their heads above dry leaf litter, like slender umbrellas blown inside out. Their thread-like stems are so delicate, it is a wonder they can push their way through the undergrowth and stones. A huge purply-blue periwinkle straggles down the slopes. By the water there are white flowers: a tall saxifrage. The slender stem is erect, ending in a six-branched head of flowers. Each branch holds seven little white flowers, birthday candles. Wrens, great tits and blue-tits sing among the tall cypresses and old, old olives with blackened trunks. On a flattish margin to the

stream, ferns unfurl and by a mossy boulder there is a parade of orchids with pale pink feathery heads, *Orchis italica*; and *Ophrys sphegodes*, the orchid with flowers the shape and colour of bees.

Higher, above Azogires, swallows dive over an exposed hill. Sheep graze among blazing yellow broom and yellow asphodel. The lambs among them are simply small-scale sheep, unlike the lambs of other breeds which are quite a different shape from ewes. These miniature sheep tittup along with heads down like small girls in their mothers' high heels. A shepherd drives along the track in a pick-up as blue as the great arc of sky. At once the sheep flock to where he stops. He catches one, ropes it and leads it to a nearby carob tree where he ties the rope. Slowly he returns to the truck. The flock gathers close as he whistles and throws down hay. He returns to the tree and kills the sheep. He hoists the sheep over a branch to hang, after cutting off its head. His knife flashes in the sun. Half the skin hangs loose. Now it is off and folded neatly. The flock browses unconcernedly all around.

On the brow of a more distant hill lies ancient Elyros. Chips of black-painted pottery lie among camomile, red anemones and orchids. The land drops sharply to deep valleys, ringed by high mountains and joined to this ring on one side only, where the unsigned track approaches from the village of Rodhovani. Down this narrow neck of land stormed Saracens in the ninth century. They overran Elyros, which had been south-western Crete's major town since Minoan times. A row of teeth grin from an exposed bank, several feet below the grassy surface. Sheep or Saracen?

From this high and beautiful spot, the beach of Souia is just visible in the V of descending mountains. Here Yorgos can no longer swim. The caves at one end have been taken over by foreigners who like to spend the summer days unclothed. Yorgos, first encountered when he was harbour master on Sifnos, explains his confusion. In his pleasant house in Hania, for he has achieved his ambition of working in his homeland's major harbour, he mourns the loss of one of his childhood's favourite haunts. The public nudity of the foreigners is offensive and embarrassing. Like the ninth century's Saracens, they have overrun the local way of life.

The village of Souia, inland from the beach, is easily missed. The new road sweeps through it fast. Yorgos' magnificent father, nicknamed the slowcoach, has died. After a year's mourning, Yorgos' mother went off to visit her daughter in Australia, virtually her first trip away from the village. She now wears smart, blue-framed Australian spectacles and her sunny face is wreathed in smiles. The old days were hard.

Stream-beds are favourite places for the two members of the periwinkle family, Nerium oleander *and* Vinca. *The pink flowers of the oleander that appear in June are smaller on the Cretan form. While* Vinca minor, *the lesser periwinkle, is common throughout Greece,* Vinca major *is native in only a few areas, mainly Corfu and Crete.*

Just below the snowline above the plain of Omalos bright blue Scilla bifolia *flowers in late March among* Crocus sieberi var. sieberi, *the form local to Crete.*

The palm forest near Vaï

In the height of summer, the island seems closer to the sun than anywhere else in Greece. Along the northern slopes of the mountainous background and on the northward-facing coast the temperature is tempered by the sea breezes of the Aegean. But on the southern coast, shut in from the north by the mountains, one feels caught on a ledge between sky and sea and exposed to a sun of African intensity. Eggs will fry on stones, they say. Should there be a wind, it will more likely be a sirocco, a hot parching wind from the south that sometimes even brings red desert dust to fall on the stony slopes of yellow thistles.

Now, in spring, a strong sirocco blows, stirring the sea into long, high lines of rollers which crash foaming on the sandy beach near Vaï. Here, a palm forest, conserved and fenced, lies like an oasis behind the rock-fringed sand. The trees are a wild date palm, thought to be indigenous to Crete: *Phoenix theophrasti greuter*. The surf, the sand, the waving fronds of the palms create a tropical scene which contrasts vividly with the shoulder of the hill that frames the view. This hillside, matted with rounded and varied shrubs, is a particularly fragrant and rich example of phrygana, the term for such communities of plants that grow on limestone slopes. Huxley and Taylor's *Flowers of Greece* mentions that 'Theophrastus in classical times was interested enough in this type of plant community to describe it, using the term we do today'. Intriguing that the palm trees below the hill bear his name – did he perhaps sit here too? The houses, towns, villages of his day may lie in ruins or beneath ploughed fields, but the phrygana he described is unchanged: rosemary, lavender, thyme, basil, marjoram and sage, and the shrubs which protect themselves with sharp thorns and prickles: thorny burnet, *Sarcopoterium spinosum*, the 'wire-netting' bush, *Euphorbia acanthothamnos*, and the hypericum that looks like miniature gorse, *Hypericum empetrifolium*.

A hillside such as this, looking today as it did in Theophrastus' time 2,300 years ago, might seem immutable. In fact, it illustrates the effect of man on the world he has taken over. Phrygana is the third stage in degeneration of an area's natural

A male Sardinian warbler, Sylvia melanocephala, *perches on a cistus bush in the hills above Vaï. This is one of the most typical birds of Greek hillsides. The jet-black head makes the male easily recognizable but the female's head is the same greyish-brown as her back. Both have white breasts and visible red eye-rings.*

vegetation. A forest of evergreen oaks and pines with an understorey of small-leaved evergreen shrubs and herbaceous perennials would have covered these low-lying hills when man first came to Crete. Gradually, over the centuries, the timber would have been cut for building and boats, and brushwood for fires. Once clearing becomes intensive, the trees have no chance to regenerate. The hillside is then covered in dense thickets of tall shrubs: arbutus, small holm and kermes oak, juniper, myrtle and tree heather, butcher's broom, terebinth and lentisc. This is maquis, which covers so many Greek hillsides in a dark green mat. It provides man with so much that is useful: gum, resin, tannin, dyes, medicines, firewood, charcoal and brushwood for penning in his goats and sheep. It is his goats and sheep, and their need for grazing, that leads to the third stage in degeneration – *phrygana*. Overgrazing and further cutting causes erosion of the soil and a barren rocky hillside. Here only briefly-flowering annuals, deep-rooted perennials, bulbs, thistles, and, in certain places, annual grasses grow. This is known as steppe.

Degeneration is the botanist's term for the process. It sounds accusing, and-derogatory of man's actions. But if we believe we have as much claim to be born, live and die in the world as any other natural form, then we can accept nature's gifts – the wood and meat for our tables and the herbs for our meat – with gratitude. True degeneration occurs only when we do not understand the results of our actions, and exploit our habitat beyond the point of regeneration.

The palms that grow behind the sandy beach near Vaï are the only indigenous palms of Greece. The climate in this eastern end of the island is hot and dry enough for this Cretan form of the North African date palm to flourish. Phoenix dactylifera *is also known as* Phoenix theophrasti, *after the philosopher who wrote a* History of Plants *in the 4th century BC.*

The Peloponnese

Someone once referred to the Balkan peninsula as the coat-tails of Europe – a graphic description of the way the land mass, where it becomes Greece and dips into the Mediterranean, disintegrates into shreds and tatters.

The Gulf of Corinth, which runs between the Peloponnese and the mainland, is more like an inland lake than the sea. In the west it narrows at the town of Patras, and the ferry crossing between Rion and Antirion takes a brief half-hour. The gulf widens as it separates the high mountain ranges of mainland and peninsula, to disappear entirely at the isthmus of Corinth. Here the land was cut away, only a hundred years ago, to form a deep, narrow canal. It is crossed by a bridge so short that it is easy to miss the quick glance down at the strip of blue water, where a large ferryboat may be slowly passing, all but brushing the perpendicular walls.

The peninsula lies on the map like a three-fingered hand, its thumb a close parallel to the final cape of the mainland where Athens and Attica meet the Aegean. At its further points north–south and east–west it is 211 kilometres long and 214 kilometres wide. But such measurements become meaningless once the bridge is crossed. The Peloponnese expands in a magic way. The soaring hulks of mountains send roads snaking from place to place, turning each into a separate country. This, and the variety of scenery and climate, convey the feeling of island travel. While snow still patches Mount Helmos in June and the large crocus *sieberi tricolor*, with pinky-purple, white and yellow bands, still flowers, all will be parched grey-grown and ochre in the deep south of the Mani, where only olives and prickly pear lend a faint colour to the barren landscape. Egrets stalk the margins of shallow Lake Pheneos, its waters shrinking in the heat, while dippers fish in the icy stream that bisects a lush green plateau 800 metres high in the mountains near Kalavrita. In the autumn, the clear pink flowers of *Colchicum boissieri*, a plant more at home in Israel and the Lebanon, shine among the stones of Mount Taïyetos. And in the shimmering heat of August, kingfishers and rock nuthatches share the same rocky cove in the Messiniakos Gulf.

Top: inland from the harbour of Ayios Nikolaos in the Mani the dark spires of cypress, Cupressus sempervirens, *rise above silvery olive groves.*

Above: high in Mount Parnon in early April the leafless branches of chestnuts weave a lattice over the view.

Opposite: Peloponnese wall lizard, Podarcis peloponnesiaca, *basks in the sun at Mistras. This ruined Byzantine town lies on a steep hillside, a paradise of spring flowers, birdsong and the buzz of insects in blossom.*

Epidavros

From Corinth a road traces the eastern outline of the Peloponnese's thumb. The land climbs steeply. On high craggy slopes, cypresses make dark green spires against sea and sky. Above Galatea, brimstones and striped swallowtails glance among bright pink rock roses and the butter-yellow flowers of rushlike Spanish broom. The ground is thick with campanulas, columbines, hummocks of bright purple vetch, pale lilac-blue scabious, mists of blue-flowered borage, and clumps of mullein, their papery yellow flowers open here and there on the growing stalks. The sun shines through the succulent russet new growth of terebinth and lights its sprays of minute scrumpled flowers.

The hillside falls steeply to the sea in a chaos of colour and birdsong. Small crescents of ivory shingle shine at the water's edge and turn the calm sea turquoise at its margin. Further out, the windless day gives the sea the colour of a moonstone. To the south, the land curls back in a narrow peninsula leading to the islands of Angistri and Aegina, and its mirror image makes a dark green shape almost as substantial as the land it reflects.

At Epidavros, umbrella pines billow above their long leaning trunks. The sun cuts dark shadows in the puffs of deep green, creating cardboard cut-outs that could be trundled on to the amphitheatre's stage as scenery.

It is school outing day. From coaches in the car park, high excited voices draw near. Then on to the stage spills a stream of brightly clothed children, shrilling like starlings. A circle coloured red, turquoise, bright blue and dark blue, emerald green and white forms in the centre for a moment, then splits like an unfurling octopus to send streamers of variegated colour running up each stepped gangway. From above, this looks like a water ballet.

Bladder campion grows from cracks in the stonework of the steps, mob caps pink with a white frill. Deep blue tassel hyacinths raise their tall bobbled heads along the stone rows of the seats. *Anemone coronaria* and *pavonina* lie like pools of blood in the ruins below. Some are small and orangey-red, others the deepest scarlet, reminiscent of Chinese silk.

High above, a buzzard mewls plaintively. Jays fly low through the pines, occasionally screeching as though in imitation of the distracted leaders of the school parties.

Two male swallowtails battle above the rocky promontory of Asini near Tolon. The swallowtail, Papilio machaon, *is a large butterfly with strongly patterned yellow and black wings tinged with midnight blue at the margin and with an orange-red circle at the base. As it breeds twice or even three times a year in southern Europe the swallowtail is a common and spectacular sight throughout Greece, in meadows and on hillsides up to 2000 metres.*

Tolon

Asini's rugged promontory, jutting into the sea to the east of Tolon's enclosed bay, is the perfect landscaped rock garden. Boulders and broken walls and stone slabs show whitish-grey between rounded hummocks of spurge in a multitude of colours. Even in April there is a hint of the parched summer to come, and some of the bushes are beginning to droop, reddish and shrivelled, while others still glisten gold and green. Waterfalls of blue campanula spill from crevices in the rock. The fluffy pink flowers of valerian lighten dark hollows and long-stemmed scabious waves ice-blue flowers among tall grasses. Swallows skim overhead, like fish cresting waves; they are surfing on currents of air. A big fat green lizard turns its tortoise-like neck, pale orange underneath, to gaze enquiringly at an intruder.

Two male swallowtails battle in the blue air, beating their striped yellow, black and white wings at each other. This makes an incongruous clicking sound. How can such fragile and beautiful creatures be so aggressive? How can such delicate wings make such a noise? Peter, sketching nearby, says butterflies are strongly territorial. Perhaps Asini, a fortified town from Early Helladic times, defended against invaders by countless populations for many thousands of years – perhaps this flowering ruin is not large enough to harbour two male swallowtails.

Myceneans, Greeks, Romans, Venetians and, most recently, Italians (a gun position bears a scratched Italian name and the date, 1942) have all looked out over this bay to the miniature wedge-shaped dark green island, where now steps lead up to a tiny white church with a red-tiled roof, guarded by cypresses. On the far side of the promontory lies a long, straight stretch of sandy beach backed by a flat expanse of orange groves burnt brown by last winter's unusual frosts. A shorter stretch of fine sand leads to the town of Tolon, which in the last twenty years has grown out of all recognition. Summer arrives early here, as the drying euphorbia and the number of visitors demonstrate.

The Balkan green lizard, Lacerta trilineata, *is the largest lizard in Greece, with a tail twice its body length. It is similar to the green lizard,* Lacerta viridis, *but can be distinguished by its broader, triangular head. A juvenile, being a darkish brown and often striped, might be mistaken for a female Peloponnese wall lizard save for the juvenile's typically large eyes and small head.*

Campanula rupestris *lights the ancient walls of Asini. There are many members of the bellflower family in a variety of habitats throughout Greece.*

The promontory of Asini at Tolon is a natural rock garden of spring flowers among yellowing euphorbia.

Our waiter sums up the character of each nationality. Greeks throw cigarette butts and napkins on the floor, and make such a mess of the table that they are a trouble to serve. Italians will steal: if the restaurant is crowded and the bill long in coming, they will slip away without paying. The Germans are good. The English are no trouble because, rather than complain, they prefer to say thank you very much and never return. The French, on the other hand, are terrific fussers. He himself moved here from Tripolis twelve years ago as the tourist boom developed. In the winter he runs a dry-cleaning business. Foreigners start arriving earlier every year. There are some who live here all year round. The landlady of a hotel lets an Iraqi live in a storeroom in the basement in return for odd jobs. Irish girls wash up in summer in exchange for meals and help pick oranges. 'I felt sorry for them,' the landlady explains. 'They told me that they came here to escape wars.'

Below the huge stone walls of Asini, on a track leading to the far beach, one of these foreigners suddenly appears. He is walking briskly as though on an errand – except that he is nude. He looks surprised. Did he not expect to meet anyone? Yet this is a public place. Might this end of the long beach be the nude area in summer? But it is not summer now, and there are middle-aged ladies who look like schoolteachers at large. One of them is sketching in the ruins above, her friend sitting beside her.

'Be careful of the holes,' says the sketcher. Concealed by the rampant undergrowth are deep round and square holes, once cisterns. 'Have you seen *Picnic at Hanging Rock?*' asks her friend. 'It's like that.'

From Astros to Sparta

The slopes of Mount Parnon above Kastanitsa are covered in thick woods of chestnut trees. In early April, the bare branches mist the hills in a tracery of a faint dusky colour that is almost lilac. Last year's leaves lie thick on the ground, and a strong wind whipping over a peak called Aleppos, patches of snow still clinging to its slopes among the firs, sends eddies down the valleys, stirring the leaves into spirals and scattering them like bits of waste brown paper.

The village is built on a rocky promontory, 850 metres high. It looks as though it has been snagged by this promontory in the act of falling from the mountains above, and hangs suspended above the steep valley. The houses, whitewashed stone with brown-tiled roofs and rickety wooden balconies, perch at all angles, one above the other. There are five children in the primary school, and a hundred or so inhabitants. But in summer it is crowded, they say. Families return home, from school and work in Tripolis and Argos and Astros, to pass the hottest weeks in the shade of the chestnuts where clear water runs in the streams.

Astros too lies on a promontory, but at sea level. On one side, a watery plain thick with reeds and tamarisk stretches from the far foothills to the scrubby margin of the sea. A long curve leads to the castle that marks the topmost point of the low promontory. The town of Astros Beach lies on the far side of the hill, above a harbour from where another long and deeper curve of sand leads towards Ayios Andreas, some 10 kilometres away. Corn buntings and cetti's warbler sing from the sprays of fluffy pink tamarisk flowers which, with the waving heads of the reed, stand in brilliant silhouette against the deep blue sky and the distant snow-capped mountains.

A road winds up into the hills. Glistening green terraces are dotted with white-blossoming almonds and pears. On the green brow of a hill a shepherd stands, his crook in sharp focus against the distant view. His flock, bells jangling, browses among the bushes. Thin red tracks lead like shining ribbons over thickly scrub-covered hills. The shepherd points the way with an expansive gesture over the wide view. But the track, after circling round several hills, leads not up into the foothills of Parnon but down to a sheltered green platform where water gushes down a crease in the hillside and a little Byzantine church stands locked in a timeless silence. It has unusually high walls for its size, and its central octagonal dome is washed

Behind the beach of Astros a cetti's warbler sings from the waving heads of common reed, Phragmites communis. *The corn bunting beyond prefers an exposed twig for its song-perch. In spring tamarisk bears sprays of pink flowers while snow still lies on the Parnon mountain range in the distance.*

alternately pink and blue, bleached by the sun. Faded frescoes are just visible through a broken pane of glass in the locked door. In the past, the door would have creaked open on to the dim and dusty interior. An alarmed bat would have sped out into the sunlight. A damp box of matches and a handful of candles would have lain in waiting on a rickety table draped in oil-cloth. It would have been possible to light a candle and say a prayer to the patron saint of the little church. In the candlelight the faded frescoes would have hinted at lost blues and golds and crimsons and greens; the sad eyes of saints would have returned a steady gaze. But too many icons have been stolen, too much damage caused. The inaccessible has become accessible and doors have been locked.

A huge bell hangs from the branch of an old, twisted plane tree which rises from the centre of a circular stone seat in the courtyard of the church. Vivid cerise-coloured cyclamen glow on the shady grassy banks of the stream, and a basin carved from stone catches the ice-cold water. There is a silent, dark movement in the bright sunlit air, and a little owl flies soundlessly away over a green meadow where pear trees stand in bridal white blossom. A tortoise crosses the path, and, hearing an approach, dives into the dense prickles of a kermes oak bush, where it stays ostrich-like, half its shell still visible, convinced it cannot be seen.

Ravens are often seen circling high above stony hillsides, their hoarse cries breaking the silence of the mountains.

A shepherd who lives in an isolated cottage not far below the church takes a lift to the nearest village where he points out the correct road for Kastanitsa and the pass across the mountains. 'Some people,' he says, 'like to mislead. They find it funny.' But, more likely, the shepherd who misdirected us thought a visit to Ayia Triadha more desirable than an attempt at crossing the pass, which is seldom used even in summer. This winter there were thirty centimetres of snow and the pass might still be blocked. He says he has five children living in Toronto where they have a lot of snow. One will return for Easter.

Beyond the village of Haradros, and over the first range of hills, the road circles down green, terraced slopes. Every so often, little streams gush down creases in the hills, and bright scarlet anemones cluster on the banks in startling contrast to the purple cyclamen among them. The road crosses a bridge at the bottom of the valley where a river rushes smoke-blue and frothing past boulders. Plane trees grow from the rocks of the river bed, their leaves just showing as faint curls of lemon yellow. Ravens circle high above. The village of Platanos spills down the side of the valley to collect in a heap above the river bank, like a stream that is dammed.

Little owls perched on a post or wall are a common sight as they are daytime hunters.

A red van full of carpets, cloths and linens from Argos pauses here. The three people crammed into the front seats wonder if the road is open beyond Kastanitsa. They have been told it is still blocked by melting snow and mud. At the next village, Haradros, they stop – no doubt calculating that they are more likely to get stuck on the mountain than they are to get good sales the far side of it. The Field Policeman, who has responsibility for 35,000 *stremmata* (3500 hectares) of land between Haradros and Kastanitsa, leads the way. He says there are many foxes and stone martens in the hills but no longer any wolves. The chestnuts which gave the village its name also give it a livelihood, from the nuts and from the wood.

There are walnuts too, and cherries in bright white flower. Spikes of iris make blue pools here and there among the hedgehog-casings of last year's chestnuts which lie thickly on the ground. Higher, the chestnut woods give way to pines, then firs – more timber for the village. A cuckoo calls, and then its voice is drowned by a

sudden rush of warm wind that sounds like an express train roaring through the high unseen mountain pass. Fragile violets nod their heads in a heap of stones by a ruined woodman's hut. Celandines gleam in the emerald green grass that marks the path of a thin clear stream as it tumbles down the terraces.

Peter paints an enormous and ancient chestnut which guards the woods. Its massive gnarled and twisted trunk, fifteen strides around, is encrusted with moss and lichen. Above a bulge near its base it has split briefly in one place to reveal what seems to be a younger tree within. This gives the impression of an arched doorway, leading to an unknown realm. Were the door to open at night, who knows what strange creatures might emerge? Beneath such a tree, it is easy to share country people's superstitions and tie a cloth to a branch to ward off evil spirits.

Higher, firs drip moss and snow lies in deep patches. Yesterday a tractor cleared the pass, and banks of snow stand high and brown on either side of deep mud. Perhaps because a fleeting appeasement was sent to the chestnut tree's spirits, our car gets through the pass. But no handkerchief, no strip of blue polythene, no talisman of any sort was tied to a branch, and there is a resounding clash.

A rock has knocked the gear rod off its socket and it is trailing in the road. Might the tin of sardines last until the next passing vehicle, and might that be in two days, or a week? How far is it down either side of the mountain to the nearest habitation, ten or twenty kilometres? But Peter has found a piece of string, a wispy length from the top of his painting haversack. By lying down, one on either side of the car, it is possible for us to reach under and, with one outstretched hand each, tie the rod against the ball-socket. After free-wheeling down several kilometres of hairpin bends, Peter gingerly pushes the gear lever into third. The knot holds and the sixty kilometres to Sparta are covered in a clutch-burning third-gear crawl. Primroses and *Anemone blanda* are passed unremarked. Not even a Parnon wolf could make us stop. When Sparta at last appears, it is not the view across its rolling green plain to the majestic barrier of Taÿetos that impresses, but the mechanic at the garage; and, later, the thriving bustle of the town itself, with its video shops and soldiers, its Italian ice-cream machines and fast-food bars, its asphalt and – its accessibility.

A marginated tortoise half-hides in a bush of kermes oak. Testudo marginata *has a distinctively flared shell.*

On the brow of a hill a shepherd stands silhouetted against the distant view of the Parnon foothills while his flock of young goats and kids browses on terraces green with spring grass.

The spreading form of the cypress, Cupressus sempervirens, *stands before a fourteenth-century church at Mistras.*

Plasterer bees swarm thickly over the arched window of a Mistras church. They are building mud nests in the mouldings.

A large tortoiseshell, Nymphalis polychloros, *a Cleopatra brimstone,* Gonepteryx cleopatra, *and a dappled white,* Euchloe ausonia, *on purple honesty and Star of Bethlehem.*

Mistras

A lower rampart of the castle that crowns the pinnacle of Mistras is reached through a burgeoning green and yellow jungle. In this sheltered hollow, the vegetation grows to an exaggerated height. Among huge bushes of euphorbia there are *Barlia*, the giant orchid with the scent of lilies of the valley, and *Ferula*, the giant fennel with sprays of leaves like asparagus fern at its base and flower heads about to burst open at the top of stems which are the height of a man. Asphodel grow from the white and terracotta shale of the crumbled walls which teeter precariously over a sheer drop on all sides of the castle walls save one.

Chunks of the lower slopes of Taïyetos have peeled away to leave ravined and thickly clad hills and exposed crags which show the wounds of this upheaval. The Byzantine town of Mistras climbs one such independent peak. The cobbled alleyways and steps between the skeletons of houses, palaces and churches make mellow patterns of pale stone and terracotta on the steep slope that faces east towards the hummocky plain of the Evrotas river. Bright red fields and symmetrical row upon row of olives make a speckled pattern far below. Gently rounded hills stretch across the horizon, with the snowy round head of Mount Parnon just appearing in the extreme distance, directly opposite.

From the base of the Mistras cliff on the western side, green meadows and the silver and dark green fuzz of olive and cypress climb towards more barren heights, dotted with firs and snow patches, and crowning the view is a peak of Taïyetos, its rocky ravines and crags appearing like fish bones beneath snow made brilliant white by the blueness of the sky.

The cobbled ways that climb steeply through the maze of ruined houses and restored churches are edged with spring flowers. There is nothing unusual here save for the profusion and the mixture of colours. The reds of anemones and the deep pinks of valerian, the paler pinks of doves-foot crane's bill and asphodel, the mauves of vetches, honesty and clovers, the yellows of marigolds, onosma, ragwort and Jerusalem sage, the white of ornithogalum, bladder campion and daisies, and the bright blues of anchusa and speedwell – all spilling over the stones, down walls, through archways, under boulders. Lizards bask on rocks: the male Peloponnese wall lizard with its breeding colours gleaming in the sun and the smaller, more distinctly striped female. Rock nuthatches, blackbirds and warblers sing in the thickets. The almond trees are already in leaf in this sheltered spot. Cypresses stand black against the distant backdrop, and here and there Judas trees billow against the sky in outbursts of breathtaking purple-pink, resonant with the buzz of insects.

Big black bees swarm thickly over walls, making mudpit homes round windows. Butterflies spread their wings on stones, and echo flower-colours in the air – lemon-yellow brimstones, dappled whites, orange tips, Cleopatra brimstones, large tortoiseshells and scarce swallowtails which every so often seem to fly backwards.

Everything is etched most sharply in colour and shape. In the arched dark windows of the ruined buildings, each white-grey stone interspersed with orange-red bricks has a clearly defined shadow. Every detail of each flower, each tree, each butterfly is set vividly against its background. Yet this clarity is softened in its final effect by the disorder of the ruins, and the rampant vegetation which everywhere has claimed Mistras for its own ends.

33

Megalopolis

About half-way between the northernmost point of the Peloponnese and the southern tip of its central prong, the town of Megalopolis lies in the centre of an undulating plain ringed by mountains. Here, a large power station fuelled by the local open-cast mines feeds the national grid and gives employment to 3000 people. A village near the town is being demolished to open up fresh mines. Who can mind moving when the new industry provides such a good living?

Not far from this modern landscape is the miraculous church of Ayia Theodora. The road to Vastas leads through low oak forests into the hills. Tree heather and Spanish broom are in flower; the air is laden with a sweet honey smell. In the village of Isaris a church bell tolls, a pause between each phrase of three, infinitely mournful. It is Good Friday. Three skinned lambs hang from hooks beneath a balcony. The stone-built houses sit firmly against the hillside, facing the sun, with views down to Kalamata and the sea. Higher still, the map of the Peloponnese is confirmed. Its three prongs stretching southwards are all visible from this high point. Far to the east, the rounded pate of Parnon and its lesser peaks lie in a faint violet line behind the jagged line of Taïyetos, while the western side of the bay of Kalamata is marked by the receding hummocks of Messinia Messi.

Three jays lead the way down a wooded valley, where bright yellow bunches of mistletoe hang from oaks. A narrow bridge crosses a fast-flowing little river, yet only a short distance above the river-bed is dry. This is a place of pilgrimage. Eleven large holm oaks, the tallest about 10 metres high, and several younger ones, grow from the roof of a minute stone-built chapel. According to legend, Ayia Theodora was murdered. Her hair turned to trees, and her blood to water. Springs rise under her church and immediately form a river. It flows in a waterfall under the bridge and away past mossy boulders down the oak-wooded valley. When there is an earthquake, they say, the river runs blood. The earth nearby is a purply red.

But where are the roots of the trees? The church of Ayia Theodora holds a small copse on its roof. Inside, many candles are lit today. Crusty blackened and pinky-brown plaster covers the roof and walls. Some patches are smooth and mottled grey and black, once frescoed. There is no sign of a single root, though a few stray wisps like dried grass-stems wave from a crack. Outside, a twisted trunk pushes into, or out of, the stones above the lintel, only to disappear entirely inside. Logic dictates the sequence of events: leaf litter deepening on the stone-slabbed roof, seeds growing into saplings, then into trees, the roots finding their way down the walls in cracks between the stones. Continuous plastering of the inside of the church over the centuries would force the roots along this path. Yet logic has no place here. The trunks rise from a thick undergrowth of butcher's broom and stunted kermes oak. Cyclamen grow among ferns. The little grey church seems to have grown from the river bank, raising its roof of trees with it.

Beside the church, orchids grow on a grassy bank. Wall lizards dart and chase each other over smooth grey rocks, raising orange throats when they momentarily pause. They make sudden rustling explosions in crisp brown leaf litter. There is another lizard which is a palish mid-brown with little rough, raised scales on its back. Planes and walnuts lean over the river-bed, where grey wagtails dip their tails on boulders and fresh-water crabs scuttle under pebbles.

Here, it is easier to believe in miracles than in nature – or rather, nature is the miracle.

In the hills north-west of Megalopolis the church of Ayia Theodora is a place of pilgrimage. According to legend Theodora was murdered, whereupon her hair turned into trees and her blood into water. A small copse of seemingly rootless holm oaks grows from the church's roof, and springs under the foundations create an instant river.

The Greek algyroides, Algyroides moreoticus, *is a pale brown lizard of the Peloponnese and Ionian islands with pointed, keeled scales.*

Vassae

Vassae has an inherent silence. Though kids bleat in a nearby flock and birds sing, a silence rings the site as though it sits within a glass bell.

It is reached from Andritsena, a village of splayed red-tiled roofs, so neatly structured from a distance, but such a tortuous winding of alleyways within; wooden houses, balconies, shuttered shops. Views from saddles high in mountains look north towards Patras and snow-peaked Erimanthos. To the south, the jagged teeth of Taïyetos are just visible, and still the rounded pate of Parnon far to the east.

The wind is chill, like a draught of spring water. The ancient site of Vassae stands 1600 metres above sea level.

Two crows rise from their mule-back perch.

Among the white rocks of the hillside and the fallen blocks of stone, there are clusters of *Anemone blanda* and bright blue periwinkle, mists of speedwell, celandines. The temple stands composed and solid even in its ruin, its pillars slightly greyer than the hillside stone. A flock of sheep browses the terraces below the temple, black-patched heads to the ground as they crop the low mat of grass and flowering weeds, their long, shaggy wool a stage of white between that of the rocks and the temple's pillars. They have curled horns and spaniel ears. There are a few goats and several kids in the flock. The kids skip from rock to rock, and try to climb a large mossy-trunked crinkle-branched oak. The shepherd throws a stone now and again to keep the flock together.

Bright yellowy-green wasps hang in the air, occasionally swooping down and forward or back like the bow of a violin, making a similar wiry twang.

Beyond the valley and hills, directly below the southern slopes, rises the peak of Mount Ilias, on the far side of which lie Vasta and the little church of Ayia Theodora. One of the hooded crows that patrol this hillside could fly there in ten minutes. By road it is an hour-and-a-half.

Two crows perched on a mule's back peel away into the air with heavy wings.

A flock of sheep browses the terraces below the temple of Apollo Epikourios at Vassae high on the slopes of Mount Paliavlakitsa. In April the valonia oaks, Quercus macrolepis, *are leafless but the ground beneath is blue with speedwell and periwinkle,* Vinca minor.

Olympia

After the night's thunderstorm, pools of water lie on the paths of ancient Olympia. The sun is breaking through heavy black clouds and highlighting here and there the dark backdrop of small, rounded hills. Tall pines rise from long grass in avenues, echoing the verticals of fluted pillars. A mass of Judas trees lays a band of pink behind the trunks of the pines: brilliant cerise umbrellas dripping blossom over the grey ruins.

Huge blocks of columns, indented and scored and scrolled, lie in lines like giant sticks of barley sugar sliced in chunks. Massive drum column bases sit tilted, like up-ended millstones with crinkled edges. In the limestone, there are fossils, shell prints, encrusted, riddled, mossy. Little rock plants grow from them. Feathery grass heads show yellow – evidence of weed-spraying. A tall fallen pine lies in the grass like a column. Rings in its trunk where it has been sawn off tidily show it was 88 years old. The bark looks like neat stacks of slate-greys, blues and patches of a pale terracotta and mauve.

Two guides sit on the steps of a temple and argue politics. There will be elections in June.

Under pine trees at the edge of the ruins of Olympia rock rose, Cistus incanus, *blossoms among bushes of broom,* Cytisus villosus.

The sun edges with a bright white line the clouds which tower over the open grassy oval of the stadium. A party of dark-clothed Greeks gathers round their guide, who speaks in the clear tones of the schoolroom about the way the games were organized. Most are paying attention, but the group breaks at the edges as men step back to take photos of their fellows.

Above the triumphal arch, which leads to the tunnelled entrance to the stadium, tassel hyacinths stud the tall grasses with bright spots of dark blue, and the folded pink flowers of convolvulus are furled like umbrellas. Asphodel bend in a breeze which ripples through the pines beyond. There is a deep, sweet honey smell from the thickets of broom and rock rose beneath the pines. The air is filled with the insistent calls of great tits and the twittering of goldfinches.

In an unkempt orange orchard on the far banks of the small rushing river Kladeos, scarlet anemones glow among the daisies and umbellifers. Frogs chorus from reedy banks. Water runs fast and sparkling over flat white pebbles. A fig tree's emerging leaves are translucent pale green, miniature on the maze of curling twigs and branches. Already figs are forming – small, shining rugger balls. Quince flowers are like rosebuds, pink-flushed white. Swallows and martins dip and dart in a continuous ballet over the river, sun catching their peachy underbellies and glossy midnight blue backs. At the water's edge there are immensely tall, waving great reed mace and tamarisk starting to flower. A cetti's warbler sings loudly, sounding angry. It is a small, nondescript brown bird, with a voice as strident as the bark of a bossy and dimunitive terrier; but the cetti insists in a rich and musical way. A nightingale sings in a dense thicket, and then flies off, shy and silent as an owl. There are cheeps and chirps, warbles, trills and whistles from every bush.

We go to sites to admire man's past prowess and work. Yet this work is in ruins, while the birds sing on. In the early spring morning, before the crowds of summer, Olympia is a work of art that has taken man and nature 3000 years to create.

Above: tassel hyacinths, Muscari comosum, *grow on a flowery bank above the Olympic stadium's triumphal arch. For over a thousand years, from 776 BC until AD 393, the Olympic Games were held every four years without a single break. Below: Olympia was the sacred precinct where wars and politics were forgotten. Today, with Judas trees in blossom among the pines, Olympia is a place where peace is almost tangible.*

Near Ayios Nikolaos in the Mani

The terraced hillsides, abandoned by people and their animals, seem at first empty and silent. In high summer, the noise of the cicadas is so incessant that it hardly registers as sound. Nor are the insects evident. Infinite numbers of them hide in the landscape, winding a million watches. Only occasionally does one appear, a dark bomber winging its way to another resting place.

One clings upside down to the branch of an olive tree. From close by the noise is piercing. Yet there is no sign of movement. The substantial insect, with mottled grey-buff head and black-and-ochre-striped body, barely distinguishable from the olive branch, does not stir. The lacy wings lie still and folded. How does it make such a sound, and why?

Further up the hillside is the smallholding of a woman who last year drove her three cows and a calf along these terraces to graze. The cows have been killed. She, living on her own, could not manage all the work. Her children are grown up and gone to the cities – Kalamata and Athens. She still has goats, and grows fruit and vegetables, and gathers olives. She is thin, wrinkled and brown, like a dry olive herself. She thinks she cannot manage the life of the hillside much longer. Soon her house too will be abandoned, and she will move down to the edge of the sea where jumbled piles of cement block will become neat rectangles for summer visitors.

In the crook of two hills near her house is a spring, a lush, green shady spot. Stone lintels make a window on to the grotto of the spring and a cup sits in a niche in the stone. The water is cool, clean and delicious. Here the woman sits for a moment with the mother of the girl her son will soon marry. The future mother-in-law has walked down from the village at the top of the hill and, being rather stout and hot, is not looking forward to the return climb. She will carry back the *dhiples* made this morning in honour of the bride and groom. The *dhiples*, crisply fried pancakes soaked in honey, follow a tradition. The couple in whose honour they were made will not. The smallholder's daughter is there too, on holiday from her work with an Athens University microbiologist. She wears a dress as cool and clean as the spring water.

A kingfisher sits motionless above a cove in the Mani. Kingfishers in Greece are as likely to be seen by the sea as by rivers. They nest in crevices or deep burrows in steep cliffs where they lay up to eight white eggs. From rocky perches by the water's edge they plunge headlong into the sea to catch fish in their long, sharp beaks.

On a further spur of the hills that descend steeply and studded with cypresses to the flat olive groves behind the bay stands a deserted village, a cluster of stone-built houses with mellow sepia-tiled roofs. The women at the spring talk of the latest empty house to be sold to a foreigner: '200,000 drachmas! Better to let his house fall in ruins than to give it away at that price.' The village is empty but for two remaining families and the life given it intermittently by the few new owners. These people raised their national flag above the village a while ago. The Greeks are tolerant, but this was too prominent a reminder of the occupation of forty years before. The flag was taken down.

In the Deep Mani to the south, where the people built tall square towers in defence against pirates and each other, the harsh rocky hillsides are burnt black. This burning of the hillsides is thought to be a protest against the government's agricultural policies, an attempt to defend a way of life.

Are the cicadas defending their territory with their incessant grating?

By contracting its muscles the male cicada vibrates drum-like abdominal membranes, thus attracting the silent female.

Below a tower which overlooks the sea near Ayios Nikolaos, a male rock nuthatch sings to his mate among the dried seedheads of Jerusalem sage. The loud, fluting call of the rock nuthatch is a common sound in the Mani. The rugged terrain suits these birds, which prefer rocks to trees for nesting and climbing.

BUTTERFLIES OF THE GREEK MOUNTAINS
These butterflies are unlikely to be seen together, but the paintings show some of the many varieties of butterflies that abound in the uncultivated mountainous areas.

Lower to middle levels With thistle, *Onopordum myriacanthum*, from left: long-tailed blue, *Lampides boeticus*; southern swallowtail, *Papilio alexanor*; eastern orange tip, *Anthocharis damone*.

High levels Shown in a mountain meadow with thistles and knapweed, from left: blue argus, *Aricia anteros*; apollo, *Parnassius apollo*; clouded apollo, *Parnassius mnemosyne*; Balkan fritillary, *Boloria graeca*; fiery copper, *Thersamonia thetis*; northern wall brown, *Lasiommata petropolitana*; (flying) dawn clouded yellow, *Colias aurorina*.

Lower to middle levels Left: two-tailed pasha, *Charaxes jasius*, the only European representative of this African family. Right: great banded grayling, *Brintesia circe*.

Towards Helmos

Driving lines of hail strike the village of Lambia, which hangs over a ravine. Shoulders of mountains, their skyline prickled with trees, recede in misty shapes, one behind the other. Streams gush down rocky slopes. A man on a mule, a slaughtered sheep across the saddle, holds a black umbrella above his head. A shepherd on a hillside has set a bush on fire and stands warming himself before it.

At the bottom of a gorge, the waters of the river Erimanthos froth grey-blue. The sides of the gorge are interlocked wedges, each a lighter shade until they merge into the cloud which reaches down into the furthest V. At Tripotamos, where three rivers meet, the bell tents of gipsies stand sodden. As the gorge widens and the hills withdraw, flat meadows of wheat, squares of dark red ploughed earth and lines of poplars edge the river bank.

In Likouria, a tiny village straddling a deep red crack in the earth, smart cars are parked. Families have returned from the cities for Easter. A man leads two brown cows tethered by their horns out of the village.

The newly-made road, well planted with saplings along its verge, leads up to the Pheneos pass. Snow lies in streaks between black firs. Clouds drip wet fingers over the distant mountains. Through the short rocky gap, there is an immediate drop to a chequered red and green plain that divides the mountain ranges of Helmos from Killini. Flood water reflects mother-of-pearl sky, and blobs of trees look like moored boats. Drifts of cloud sweep past in a sighing sound of wind and rain. The road, bulldozed in preparation for asphalt, is plasticine in red mud. At the northern end of the plain, the track leading up into the peaks of Helmos is impassable.

A cave on Helmos is one of the several places in Greece which claim to be the source of the river Styx. Guarded by dragons, the mythological Styx is the main river of the underworld, the land of the dead. The flowers that grow by the cave entrance, dampened by the spray from a waterfall above, must be seen later in the year, in May or June. Like the receding shapes of mountains in the rain, and like the magic way the peninsula expands beyond its size, Helmos has receded from this journey to the next.

The Gulf of Kalamata

In the Gulf of Kalamata, the sea stretches flat and empty, a pale membrane pulled tight at the horizon in a curve that echoes the prow of our boat. To the east lie the misty shapes of land rising steeply to Taïyetos. The mountains, violet-shadowed and parchment-coloured, are skeletal, a heap of bones scoured clean with a stiff steel brush and left to bleach in the sun. The Mani stretches south, appearing from this distance as untouched as it was before the road was built. Though it looks as empty as the sea, there will be traffic on that twisting scar of road: backpackers and loaded motorbikes, caravans, the summer's tail-end of tourists. From this distance there is no hint of them.

Nothing stirs the milky surface of the sea but a few pleats tugged blue by a soft south-westerly. Before the road was built, the Gulf was a highway. Caiques plied between the villages of the coast. Cargo ships crowded the harbour of Kalamata, taking raisins and olives and cigarettes to Athens. Now giant articulated trucks fill

The heart-shaped orchid, Dactylorhiza cordigera, *is one of the many rare species of flower that grow on Mount Helmos. Such flowers should be admired but never picked: their numbers are declining rapidly.*

Feeding on origanum, with a carline thistle in the background, are three butterflies of the lower to middle mountain levels. Left: spotted fritillary, Melitaea didyma meridionalis. *Centre: Balkan marbled white,* Melanargia larissa. *Right: Lang's short-tailed blue,* Syntarucus pirithous.

Swordfish, Xiphias gladius, *were seldom hunted in the past. With the increased demand for fish and depleting stocks many fishermen now specialize in catching them.*

A turtle dove chased by Eleonora's falcons finds safety on a life-belt. Turtle doves are frequently the target for hunters' guns, but this dove considered humans less dangerous than falcons.

the wide cobbled quay before the imposing harbour master's offices. Lorries can make the deliveries to the rest of Greece and abroad in a fraction of the time. The harbour water is clean. Fish, grey mullet and saupe, can be seen in its clear depths. Men and boys sit for hours holding lines over the water. A short distance from the lighthouse, a large swordfish rises in a flashing arc from the water. Once, twice, three times, it arches itself above the surface, a metallic bow. And a few moments later a pale green submarine shape appears beside the boat, dives under and disappears. It is as long as the boat is wide, two metres and more: perhaps it was a tunny or a shark.

Ships now draw a line well to the south of the Peloponnese's three prongs. On the distant rim of the sea's blue circle, they look like the pieces of some modelling toy, segments of a city, belfries, steeples, apartment blocks, telegraph poles, being pulled along to form a new floating city, a modern Venice in a further invisible circle of blue. The Venetian forts of Methoni and Koroni, the dun-coloured towers of the Mani peninsula and the walled town of Monemvassia guard their peninsulas uselessly.

Monemvassia on its lump of red rock is held to the land by a thin cord of causeway. From the sea, it looks as though it is pinned to the rock, held in place by its apron of wall, as one-dimensional as a child's drawing of a town. Twenty or so years ago it was all but deserted, its houses in ruin. It might have become another Mistras, the skeleton of a town, foundation walls appearing through undergrowth. But the late twentieth century has taken Monemvassia under its wing in its own way. It has made it fashionable to turn a crumbling house into a holiday home. Stout wooden doors boast brass knockers. Cleverly hinged shutters hang over windows and antique lace inside them. Geraniums and plumbago cascade over steps. There are ice-cream parlours and restaurants, and shops selling garish pottery, jewellery and 'local' crafts brought from Athens for the season. A brand-new loom sits on view in one cottage-shop. The causeway is rebuilt. A road climbs to the arched entrance to the old town. On the mainland, the new town grows up the hillside. Where have all the locals come from, to serve the tourists? 'Crete, Thessaloniki, and from the villages in the hills,' someone explains. 'At the end of October, we go home and pick olives.' This place is as unconnected with reality as the child's drawing it resembles from the sea. Yet it is the only kind of reality that such a place can have when its original fortress function is no longer valid. Better this than a ruin, perhaps.

At Porto Kaio, on the south-eastern coast of the Mani, the squat towers of a deserted monastery are pinned to the rugged hillside by walls in much the same way as Monemvassia but on a tiny scale. Cypresses stand upright in a crease, a dim reminder of the northern and gentler Mani. From Ayios Nikolaos southwards, the peninsula broods above the sea like some enormous and forbidding lion. The cliffs on the southern cape are abrupt and racked. Porto Kaio is an oasis of safety, a sheltered enclosed anchorage. At night the bay is a riot of fish rising, a continuous plop and splash, rings spreading in the moonlit water. A myriad fish seem to be battering the sides of a boat as though urgently tattooing a request to enter. In the morning, four sardines are found dead but still gleaming on the deck. They had been chased by garfish and jumped to safety – only to die.

Five hours out from Monemvassia, the wind rises. Within half an hour, the calm blue surface of the sea is whipped into waves. Within another, it is impossible to hold course for Milos. Wall after wall of water sends the prow high to the sky, then down to a sickening depth. To the north-east, into the wind, there appears a small hummock of rock, and after a two-hour struggle against the sea, its lee is reached. Two hundred metres high and perhaps two kilometres in area, it rises sheer from the sea, but on its southern face there is a small stretch of shelving sand in which to anchor. This is Falconera, a godsent haven in one of the most open stretches of the Aegean. The falcons which give the rock its name mewl and squeak and skitter, plane, swoop and dive around the cliffs. All day long they keep up a continuous activity and conversation. They are nesting, and Peter explains that they nest at this time of year, September, because they can feed off migratory birds. A greenfinch appears over the cliffs at this moment, living evidence. At once three falcons are there. One, with a twist and a flick, catches the finch and bears it away up the cliff, pursued by the other two falcons, squeaking and mewling in frustrated anger. To think that this small finch journeyed so far from the north, crossed such a stretch of sea, to shelter and rest for a while on this haven of rock, only to be devoured the moment it arrived ... like the sardines that jumped to safety and death, and very possibly, though awful to contemplate, like the travellers who found shelter here, only to run out of food and water before the wind dropped ...

Four falcons give chase, squealing excitedly across the face of the cliff. A small grey bird beats its wings furiously to escape. The hunt circles the sandy beach, disappears behind the rocky edge. A moment later there is the scuffle of wings on board, and a turtle dove flops exhausted on to the inner rim of, appropriately enough, a life-belt. It has taken the chance that humans are less dangerous than Eleonora's falcons. It swings with the rocking of the boat in its life-belt, as safe from the falcons as a budgie in a cage from alley cats. The falcons mewl crossly from the cliff but will not come close. The turtle dove stays on board all through the afternoon, moving to a better perch on a rope handrail, occasionally letting its eyelids close in a brief siesta over its glistening tawny buttons of eyes, craning its neck forwards and backwards to balance the swell. As the sun sets it moves to the boom, where it stretches a leg beneath a fluffed-out wing, ruffles its feathers and pecks them with a beak the colour and shape of the sharpened lead of a pencil. When the sun has set and the falcons have fallen still and silent on the backdrop of cliff, the turtle dove slips away unseen over the sea to the south.

Eleonora's falcon occurs in two colour forms: grey-black and, more common, light grey with streaked reddish underside. It is the only autumn-breeding bird of Europe. The falcons nest in colonies on cliffs in the paths of migration so that they can feed their young on the birds they catch. It is estimated that about 3000 pairs, over half the world population, breed in the Aegean but numbers are declining due to human predation.

The Cyclades

Top: Plaka, the capital of Milos, seen from the little chapel of Prophitis Ilias, with sea squill in the foreground.
Above: in spring the rounded, terraced hillsides of Sifnos are filled with flowers.

Opposite: a golden oriole, on its northward migration, rests on a fig-tree branch on Sifnos. The village of Castro appears in the distance.

There is a memory test in which objects are placed on a tray, then covered, and a list made of them. By closing the eyes and summoning to mind the blue sea and the grey shapes that lead from horizon to horizon, it is possible for us to list 65 of the islands inhabited by a hundred or more people. We know 37 of these, which leaves 28 unvisited on our memory's map and more in reality. They say there are 1,500 Greek islands altogether, which must include not only the little islands with very few inhabitants, some of which we know, but also every single rocky islet where only birds can land.

However much time is spent travelling in Greece, there is always another island on the horizon, beckoning. The Cyclades, the largest group, are the most teasing for travellers. The islands lie not only in chains, like the Ionians, Sporades and Dodecanese, but in circles too. From the doorstep of every Prophitis Ilias, the chapel built on an island's highest peak, two or more other islands can be seen, lying like unanswered questions on the rim of the encircling sea.

The name Cyclades means 'circling ones', the sacred island of Delos having been considered the pivot in ancient times. They are also known as the Dry Islands. The typical image is of a rugged barren lump of land with stone-walled terraces, ochre thistles and a scattering of villages and churches, where the sun plays a blue geometry on centuries of whitewashed stone. But this is only part of the picture. With the first autumn rains, the islands gradually turn green. In spring, the colours and varieties of wild flowers make gardens of the hillside terraces. There are springs hidden in mountain creases and in valleys, where even in August water flows in gullies thick with vegetation and croaking frogs. Migratory birds rest here, in olive groves and vineyards. A Cycladean island in April or September is the best place to watch bee-eaters and rollers.

Because of the way the islands were formed when vast upheavals split them from the Balkan peninsula and from each other, the wildlife is distinctive. There are species of flora and fauna which have died out on the mainland but continue to flourish in the islands, and others which, because of an island's isolation, have formed new species entirely. Some islands have no poisonous snakes; others, no scorpions. Kithnos and Serifos are the only places in Greece where you can see in May a particular species of fritillary, *Fritillaria tuntasia*. The lizards of Milos, Kimolos and a few small neighbouring islets are a separate species, with their own distinctive markings. Here too there is the blunt-nosed viper, a snake found only in the western Cyclades. An agamid lizard, common in Africa and Asia, also appears in small colonies in Greece: around Thessaloniki in the north, on Corfu in the north west, and on a few of the central Cyclades – Mikonos, Delos, Paros, Antiparos and Naxos. With its large head, stocky body and long thin tail, it is known locally as the little crocodile.

Milos

There is no shelter from the wind that circles the little chapel on its peak. From every direction the wind carries sounds. From the sea far below and the harbour of Klima, the voices of two men in a boat are as clearly audible as the shouts, calls and conversations from the village of Plaka perched on its rocky promontory above the chapel, and the lower village of Tripiti that sits in the lee of a windmilled brow to the south. 'Mama! Mama! Where are you?' The call is so clear that it seems possible to provide the answer in an ordinary conversational tone: both mother and daughter are visible from this vantage point, one on a balcony, the other in a nearby courtyard.

On the descending stubble terraces below the chapel, the figures of three foreigners have appeared. For some time and at a distance from each other, they wander this way and that – stopping, staring, turning, climbing higher, scrambling lower, now this way, then that. After a while, one figure stumps off up the winding road to Tripiti. His red shorts make him look hot and cross. A girl in blue shorts comes across a pillar in a field. She bends over it, circles it, walks away, and then returns to bend over it once more. Perhaps they are looking for the ruins of the theatre. These lie only a few terraces below, yet are invisible to them.

The chapel is open. This is unusual nowadays. Islanders have learnt that there are people who steal ikons. Inside, wicks are lit in jars of oil and the tiled floor is washed clean. The smell of sunbaked oilcloth and faded incense is evocative of the days when the door of every Cycladean chapel was kept unlocked. In this one, only the icon of Ilias may be older than the century. In his glass case the saint looks lugubrious. The mouth, set at the bottom edge of the traditionally elongated face, has one corner turned down. This gives him a look of despairing disgust, as though at the garland of white tulle and plastic flowers hung around the frame. No doubt the whitewashed plaster on the walls hides frescoes. It is an ancient church, built on the site of a temple. Sections of pillars jut from the outside walls, as thickly whitewashed as the stones.

After a time away from the Cyclades, the blinding light is a striking and fresh surprise, and to make Milos the first of these islands heightens the impact of the light. The villages of Milos are no whiter than any other Cycladean village and messier than many, but the earth of the island is white and laid bare. Volcanic activity has left the island rich in minerals and ores; kaolin, bentonite and perlite are mined here. The hills look as though they are suffering from some scalp disease. Every low hill that forms the rim of the huge circular bay, the crater of a volcano, has its bald white patch. Yet the rocks that jumble the steeply terraced slopes around Prophitis Ilias' chapel are a purply grey, the colour of the stems of the sea squill

The Milos wall lizard is found on only a few Cycladean islands: Milos, Kimolos and the uninhabited islets of Antimilos, Falconera and Velapoula. Podarcis milensis *is a small lizard; adults may reach 6.5 cm from snout to vent, with a tail of twice that length. The male has a faintly striped brown back and black flanks, throat and cheeks with well-defined bluish-white spots. The pattern on the paler female is less distinctive.*

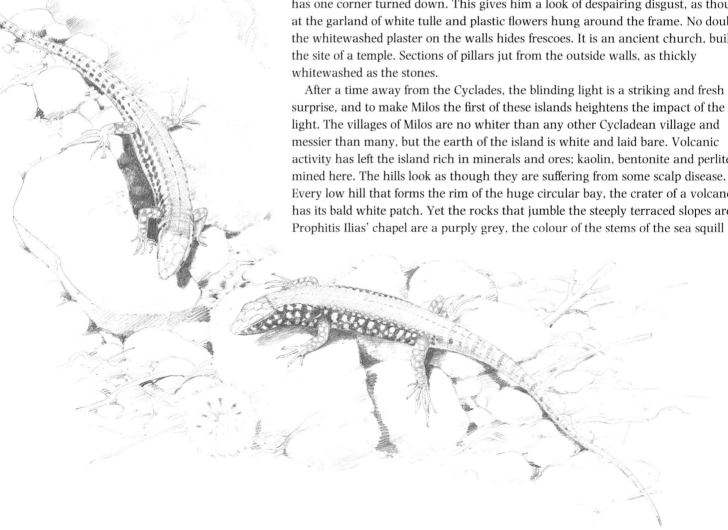

which have sprung into flower and which bend with the wind against the view.

    The wind and the sounds it carries immediately cease in the cradle of the amphitheatre. It is set in such a way on the curve of hillside that from the tiers of marble seats there is no view but of the stage and its backdrop of bay and the hills on the distant shore. Two cicadas cease their chirping and the theatre encloses a perfect half-sphere of silence. On the stage, a lizard slips between dried grasses. Unaware of spectators, it pauses and lifts a foreleg in a rapid movement as though scratching its head in thought. A metre or so away, an ant approaches carrying a husk of grass seed. It is as unaware of the lizard as the lizard is of the spectators. A second later the ant has disappeared. All that remains is the grass seed beside which the lizard flicks her tongue. She is a female wall lizard, slimmer, smaller and with less sharply defined markings than the male.

Reminders of the island's long history lie
among the olive trees on the hillside below
Plaka and Tripiti: polygonal walls,
Christian catacombs and an ancient Roman
theatre. The drawing shows sea squill
growing in the theatre among marble blocks
with beautifully worked palmettes and
anthemiums.

Despite the general pollution of the Mediterranean, the Aegean is still relatively clear. Common fish of rocky shallows are (left) painted wrasse with male and female Turkish wrasse in front; (centre, by rock) comber; (right) two-banded bream. In the background is a shoal of damsel fish, descriptively called 'nuns' in Greek.

The blunt-nosed viper, Vipera lebetina, *is found only on Milos, Sifnos and a few other western Cycladean islands. Its colour is very variable: from dark to light brown or grey, depending on sex, age and season. It is usually larger than the nose-horned viper of other areas of Greece,* Vipera ammodytes. *Both are highly venomous.*

At Phylakopi, a male wall lizard circles Peter's feet as he sits painting. The greyish-black and white mottled pattern beneath the lizard's throat is vivid, and echoes the colours of the island's earth. This lizard is found only on Milos and a few nearby islands, and no doubt its particular markings developed in response to a need for camouflage. Just in front of Peter's feet, the ground drops away. A giant keyhole has been formed and at the bottom there is an oval of sea lapping at a handkerchief of sand. Steps have been cut in the chalky rock and it is possible to clamber down. The walls of the keyhole look as though they have been made by someone who was forced to use a great deal of white cement to keep his stone wall upright. At the far end the sea enters through a low archway. The whole headland seems about to cave in. The ancient city of Phylakopi straggles half in, half out of the sea. Its maze of stone walls started toppling down 3000 years ago and is still toppling. There are caves, both natural and man-made. Both man and the sea have been busy digging into Milos for such aeons of time that any view is transient. When Phylakopi was abandoned as the main city of the island, the new city grew between Plaka and the sea, and now that too lies tumbled beneath the earth. In 1920 a farmer ploughing in a field near the early Christian catacombs felt the ground caving in beneath his plough. The earth fell away and revealed a statue – the Venus de Milo which is now in the Louvre.

Twenty years after our first visit here, the port of Adamas is scarcely recognizable. The caique captain who brought us here, having delivered his melons to Sifnos,

now runs a large hotel and a boat that takes tourists on day-trips round the island.

'Twenty years?' echoed the grocer, as amazed by this length of time as if it had been 3000. 'You'll see how the place has changed, and for the worse. No fish, and all tourists. The locals, all dead. In another twenty years, I'll be dead too.' He was convinced that the foreign girl who had just left the counter had been trying to cheat him. She was equally convinced that he was trying to cheat her. Neither was the case; it was simply a misunderstanding, a lack of communication.

They say the farmer was given an overcoat in exchange for the Venus de Milo. In those days, he may well have been pleased, unaware of a statue's value.

Nowadays it is snakes that are being taken from the island. It is thought that over a thousand are removed each year. This year a young German hoped to make away with 70 live vipers of the island's endemic sub-species. He would have sold them for an estimated 20,000 Deutschmarks, about £5000. No doubt he was confident that no islander would object to the removal of the snakes they stone to death; nor would an islander have any idea of their value. But, like the lizard in the theatre, he had been watched. Acting on information supplied by three foreign conservationists, and with the co-operation of the Forestry Service, the local police detained him and confiscated the snakes under Greek wildlife protection law. The snakes were returned to different parts of the island. Might the statue of Venus one day make a similar return?

Milos, formed by volcanic activity, is an island of hot springs, strange rock formations and rich mineral and ore deposits. Obsidian made the island important in ancient times. Minerals are still the island's main resource: perlite, bentonite, barium, kaolin, sulphur, manganese and silicates are mined. The chalky white rock lends itself to tunnelling, by both the sea and man. The painting shows the coast near Phylakopi where there are as many man-made rock dwellings as there are natural caves.

From Kimolos to Sifnos

The date 1865 is carved on the wooden wheel that once turned the millstone. Potter wasps fly in and out of holes where pegs used to fit. On a newer beam, 1939 is painted in red.

The six windmills stand on the skyline above the harbour of Kimolos in varying stages of ruin. Across the rockstrewn hill, low stone huts appear above stone walls, black squares of windows distinguishing them from the landscape. Bushes of prickly pear look like jumbled piles of green and yellow stones. A man in a wide-brimmed straw hat, riding a donkey and leading two others, moves slowly through the maze of walls, following a path. The island lies heaped below, a line of loosely folded sedge-brown hills hiding the misty sea on all sides save the southern. Today there is no wind and the sea is still. Not a wave breaks on the edges of the mouse-shaped islets that lead the eye to the crumbling white cliffs of Milos. Poliagos, where not long ago a few families still lived, lies to the east, a violet cut-out pasted between sea and sky.

The main village stands just below the mills, but no sounds rise from there. Most of the summer visitors have returned to their homes and jobs in Piraeus and Athens. The mines of Kimolos provide work for only 15 islanders. A good three-quarters of the husbands and fathers are in the Merchant Navy. The 600 permanent inhabitants depend for their livelihood on the outside world. Early this morning a caique brought melons and tomatoes from Pollonia, the village on Milos that lies across the narrow straits. A Kalimnos caique left at dawn, the four sponge fishermen on board continuing their journey home with the strings of sponges they had collected off the south coast of Crete. At each overnight stop on the journey, they work on the sponges. With heads bent, shoulders hunched and hands in a line on the rail, they tread the sponges, their feet moving in a slow dance. After many such poundings and washings in sea water, the sponges can be packed tightly in boxes and sacks. At each harbour, a few are tossed into a shallow basket and dumped on the quay. On being asked the price, the captain says, 'Choose one and I'll tell you.' A fat, clean springy sponge, smelling faintly of the sea, costs 300 drachmas. These men dive to 10 metres or so. Others from Kalimnos dive, with oxygen bottles, 30 or 40 metres. Bright red wetsuits hang from the mast, boom and rails, incongruously sporting beside the wiry and wizened bodies of the aging men. The youngest member of the crew, fair-haired, has only one hand.

The gaunt skeletons of windmills mark many a skyline in the Cyclades, like the tombstones of a self-sufficient way of life. No longer is island-grown wheat ground into flour by these mills. Progress – the coming of electricity, and faster, more frequent boat services – has made island life easier, but for fewer people. Sadly, progress leads to rural depopulation.

A sponge is the fibrous skeleton of a low form of animal that lives in warm seas to depths of 200 metres.

There are small colonies of one species of agamid lizard in Greece, mainly on the central Cyclades. This is Agama stellio, *called 'little crocodile' in Greek.*

In the tiny harbour's café, every conversation is shared. 'Snakes? The island's full of them. Adders. Though there aren't so many as there were. Germans come collecting, and take them away in bags. I don't know why.'

From the mills above the village of Kimolos, the sea looks as flat as glass, but wisps of cloud begin to form over the distant humps of Milos, Poliagos and the hills of Kimolos itself. Sifnos, a vague shape on the northern horizon, begins to recede into a misty band. Such fragments of clouds look innocuous but could well mean another bout of *meltemi*. In the village, people tell us that the radio forecasts a force 8 wind. By the time the boat has cleared the northern cliffs of Kimolos, the outline of Sifnos, although much closer, has disappeared, and the glassy surface of the sea is crumpled. An hour later, with the steep shoulders of Sifnos comfortably hunched on the beam, the *meltemi* from the north has corrugated the sea, and on each ridge white caps form as though the stuffing is coming out.

In Kamares harbour a line of yachts forms; six, then eight, then ten, shoulder to shoulder. Nikolakis' large caique returns from sword-fishing before planned. He, too, has heard the forecast. The quay becomes a network of ropes and anchor lines as the wind rises. In the night the storm starts. Gigantic gusts of wind explode down the steep mountain walls of the bay, and shoot in from every direction. Along the quay there are rattles, shakes, cracks, slaps, creaks, groans – each noise so loud that it seems the final emergency. And then there's a lull and a gentle enough rocking before the next series of explosions.

The morning's sun makes the continuing storm less of a monster. A series of visitors comes on board *Moby Dick*, friends made in the past and the children of children we knew. Costas, the 12-year-old son of Evangelio who sang us the May song when she herself was that age, watches a seagull fly past. 'That's my uncle's,' he says. The explanation for this puzzling remark is that his uncle, the fisherman Nikolakis, had mended the gull's broken wing, nursed and fed it, and now it goes fishing with him, perched on the mast, or following behind. Costas tells us that the largest swordfish his uncle caught this year weighed 190 kilos.

In the evening, Nikolakis comes on board for a beer, joining the two cousins who share the name of Costas Paleos. Soon there is a heated discussion. Costas, once a potter, agreed to let a converted pottery to someone from Thessaloniki. It is now a disco playing music until all hours of the night. There have been complaints, and visits from the police. Costas, as landlord, is worried; what is he to do? Nikolakis considers he should have been more careful in his choice of tenant.

'We've got to take care all the time. We've got to know when to stop building more and more places for visitors, more and more cafés and restaurants and shops.' His eyes flash and dart like fish as he bangs the table with a fist. 'Here on Sifnos we now have everything we need. We have buses going up and down all day, we have roads, electricity, clean beaches.' Forks jump on the table. 'When people congratulate me and say how beautiful the place is, how clean, how tidy, it doesn't mean anything to me. I don't do it for the bravos and the thanks. It's a constant fight.' He pauses to save a glass. 'It's a constant fight,' he continues, his fist slamming his knee instead of the table, iron on iron, 'to save the island from the fate of Ios and Mykonos, and I do it so that I can leave a good place for my children.'

Later another friend talks of the *agrimi* of Antimilos. 'There aren't as many as there were once. There are fishermen who take guns when they go there. They shoot the goats to eat.' But the *agrimi* are protected by law; Antimilos is a reserve. 'Huh! We Greeks and the law ... we pay no attention to the law, and the law pays no attention to us.'

High above the sea on the eastern coast of Sifnos, brilliant purply-blue flag irises make a spectacular display among the myriad spring flowers of an ungrazed terrace.

Sifnos in the spring

The narrow bay of Kamares is overshadowed by steep mountains which on the north and south plunge straight into the sea. A long stretch of sand links the harbour village, which fringes the foot of the southern mountainside, with a narrow line of dwellings and potteries drawn where the northern mountainside spills into the sea. There are times in spring and autumn when the sun sets on the sea's horizon exactly midway between the two headlands and blazes a path down the bay to the centre of the beach. It is as though nature, when creating this landscape, wished to construct a rectangular sundial.

Two decades and more ago, few lights appeared in Kamares after the sun had set. It was possible to look across the bay and give the flickering pinpricks of light names: Stavros, Boulis, Simos and Kambourakis. The lights took on the characters of the

This painting shows a pair of blue rock thrushes. The musical fluting call of Monticola solitarius *is a familiar sound near the rocky coasts of the Cyclades.*

families that ran each shop. The light that lasted longest into the winter nights was the one that belonged to Simos. Here the regulars would gather. Yorgos, the Cretan customs officer and harbour master, would leave his intermittent melancholia and records of Theodhorakis in the office next door and join in animated conversation with Nikos the deaf-mute. Nikos, gnarled hands flying above the knob of his shepherd's crook, prickly chin thrust forward, gums bared in a grin, conversed in a language that was rich and descriptive. Yorgos, Simos and Simos' daughter Aglaïa and son Lefteris understood this language well enough, but it was Simos' wife who was the best translator. Every now and then, her name would be called: 'Katé! Kiria Katé! What's he saying?' And Katé would jerk away from the wall against which she had been leaning her tired and heavy body and, wiping a yawn away from a mouth almost as toothless as Nikos', would translate. Sometimes talk gave way to music. There would be a guitar, a violin, and soon all the singers would want an instrument. The goods that hung from hooks and crowded the shelves of the shop's walls would be ransacked – saucepans and lids, wooden spoons and washboards, wire whisks and tins of dried beans, toilet paper and combs, metal spoons and tin wine jugs. There was no end to the ingenuity of the determined music-maker. Simos would pump the Tilley lamp and bring on more wine. On the walk back across the beach by moon or starlight, the well in the sand from which water was drawn to fill pitchers would be given a wide berth.

Now the village of Kamares is creeping up the mountainside. First, rooms to rent were built on the roofs; then, as children grew and married and tourists brought work, a string of additions was added in close-packed lines behind each original house. Simos and Katé have retired to a back row. Their eldest son, Nikos, runs the café at the water's edge. He has a son called Simos. In another decade, the chain is likely to move one step further up the mountainside.

The mountains, unchanged, magnificently disregard this activity at their hemline. On their time scale, it is not long since Sifnians mined gold and built a treasury at Delphi. But on our time scale, it seems an age since the occasion when a foreigner fell down one of those ancient gold-mine shafts. Nikolakis, still the main fisherman of the harbour, offers fat lobster and remembers that night of the festival of Ayios Sostis, the church built on the brink of the mines. He had been fishing off the coast. Eventually piercing whistles from shore attracted his attention. The foreigner, with a broken leg and concussion, was reached by tunnel, carried to the sea on a makeshift

In a ravine near Castro thick clumps of reeds in a stream-bed provide an ideal habitat for herons and bitterns. The little bittern, Ixobrychus minutus, *breeds in Greece but the night heron,* Nycticorax nycticorax, *in the foreground is on its way north.*

Further up the ravine, one of the many pigeon-houses of Sifnos stands on a narrow terrace above the stream-bed where oleanders and fig trees grow between slabs of rock.

53

The decline in numbers of peregrine falcons, once common throughout Europe, is thought to be caused by the increased use in agriculture of pesticides and chemicals which are transmitted in the food chain. In the Cyclades where such poisons are not widely used, peregrines are still often seen.

stretcher and taken by Nikos, Peter (for translation) and a few others (for the sheer excitement of it) to hospital on Syros.

Some years later, it was the church itself that fell down the mine shaft. It is now rebuilt in excellent Cycladean style by an architect who Smaragtha thinks might be French. Smaragtha, well into middle age, is now married into the family that takes care of the church. She and her new husband Yorgos are working today in a field below the path to Ayios Sostis. They are sowing chick peas. Yorgos drives the two cows, one beige, one white, which are yoked together to draw the single harrow through the reddish-brown earth. Smaragtha walks behind, throwing the seed into the furrows. The terraces, edged with whitish-grey rock and stone walls, descend in a bulbous curve to the glittering sea far below. Every so often, along the high cliff path, birds of prey hang momentarily overhead, or dive towards the distant sea: buzzards, kestrels, hen harriers, peregrine falcons – and Peter thinks one dark shape could be a Bonelli's eagle.

On a further slope of hillside, there is what might be mistaken for a high-walled garden. Unterraced and ungrazed, it looks as if it has been set aside purely for its flowers, not simply abandoned by its owner. It is a glowing mass of flowers: purple and yellow sage, white camomile, yellow daisies, scarlet poppies, gorse, asphodel, tassel hyacinths and, most staggering of all in their height and their intensity of colour, purple flag irises. They grow in great clumps among the boulders and Peter, perching in their midst to sketch, might almost be a garden gnome. Higher up the hillside, shaped stones lie hidden in the undergrowth in the disrupted pattern of ruined houses. A partridge, surprised, freezes momentarily on a lintel beneath bushes of Jerusalem sage, then clatters away. Though the surface ruins are of recent history, the underlying stones, in the way they are shaped, speak of a past that might reach back to the time of the gold mines. In the silence after the partridge's flight, the atmosphere seems to draw itself together again and settle thickly over this patch of hillside. It is the atmosphere of a very ancient place.

'Ruined! All is ruined! The people and the island are both ruined!' The speaker, an architect who has had a summer house in Kamares for many years, cannot be the first to utter this complaint. But it is not the exhaustion of a gold mine that is causing today's ruin. It is progress and the gold mine of tourism. He is beyond cheer. Washing-machines, put forward on the side of progress in the conversation, he dismisses out of hand. But perhaps he has never had to wash clothes and sheets by hand in icy water pulled up from a well in a strong north wind in January.

Costas, Smaragtha's brother and once our landlord, crosses the beach at dusk. He still carries drinking water in a pitcher from Kamares to the potteries where he lets out a honeycomb of rooms. From the little lake behind the beach, where freshwater turtles used to swim but which is now shrunken and choked with reeds, a purple heron rises and slowly flies across the path of the sun that is setting between the two headlands. Two egrets flap lazily between one tamarisk and another. Below the trees, the sand is churned by the tracks of lorries. There are mounds of gravel, barrels, spilt tar, piles of long black pipes, litter.

'Nothing is ever finished, everything is always in the middle. We Greeks –' Costas, the taxi-driver, breaks off in despair. The most important road, the one that runs from Kamares up the prettily winding river valley to the main villages on the crown of the island, is still not asphalted, although it was made wide enough for cars many years ago. It should have been done when the harbour was extended. Now large ferry-boats can moor at the quay. Cars and lorries crowd the island's new roads, but it has taken until 1983 for the Army to come and asphalt the main road. Costas sighs. The two faces of progress are a constant theme. He admits the dichotomy. He needs the work and the money, but regrets the loss of the peace and quiet. 'Solitude and silence! Peace and quiet!' There is an irony in hearing these words spoken with longing when once they were uttered with dismay.

Andonis, Katé's brother, has always understood the need for peace and quiet. He spends the winter in Kastro but in summer, when the invasion starts, he retreats up the ravine to his smallholding. On the walk up the ravine, where the narrow stream trickles over flat boulders and forms deep, green pools beneath thickets of giant reed mace, herons burst out of the undergrowth a few paces ahead. They rise with a tremendous clatter of wings and fly off with legs outstretched as though pointing their toes in strenuous exercise. There are both purple and night herons here, and little bitterns. Common and green sandpipers pick their way along the stream's muddy margin, where later in the year wild celery and watercress grow. The fronds of the reeds, the height of a house, reach skywards and point the direction of the wind with a gracious stiffness. Oleanders grow out of crevices in slabs of blue and grey rock where the stream cascades in little waterfalls. The hillsides rise on either side in ancient terraces. Mounds of yellow Jerusalem sage and purple-flowering sage, bushes of bright yellow-green euphorbia and glistening red and green lentisc and terebinth are heaped among outcrops of rock and terrace walls in disrepair. In the

Fed by winter rains, a stream flowing down a ravine forms a pool among reeds behind the beach of Kamares. Even in the dry months there is still enough water here to attract passing herons. The purple heron, shown in the drawing, has pinkish-purple plumage and in flight holds its head less tightly tucked into its body than does the grey heron.

FLOWERS OF THE FIELDS AND TERRACES

Before spring ploughing, cultivated fields and terraces are a mass of wild flowers of many different species. These common 'weeds', the ancestors of so many garden flowers, are increasingly rare in areas of more extensive agriculture where herbicides are used.

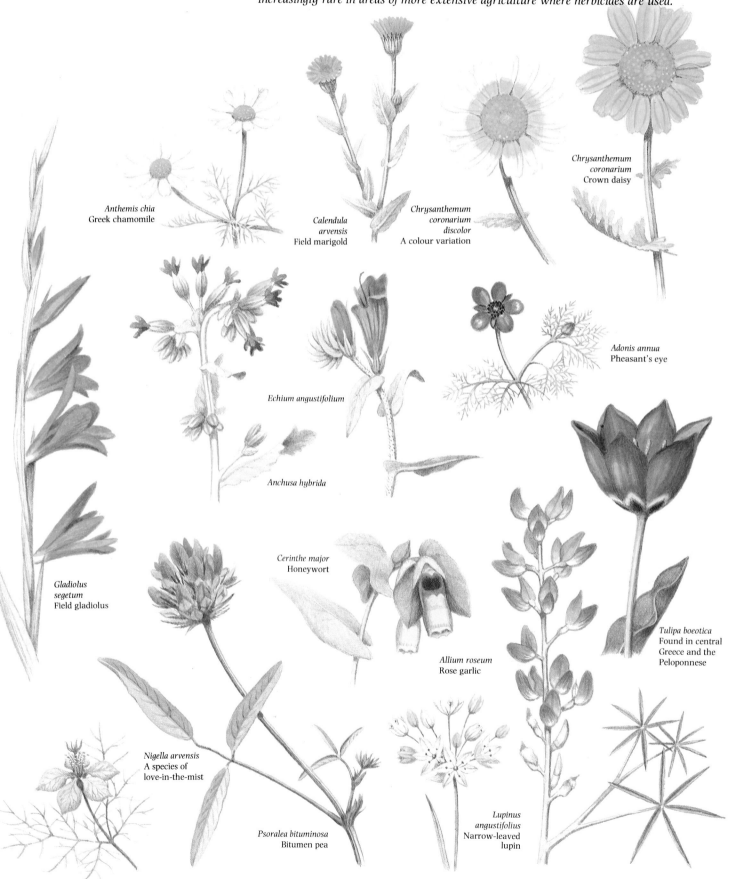

Anthemis chia
Greek chamomile

*Calendula
arvensis*
Field marigold

*Chrysanthemum
coronarium
discolor*
A colour variation

*Chrysanthemum
coronarium*
Crown daisy

Echium angustifolium

Adonis annua
Pheasant's eye

Anchusa hybrida

*Gladiolus
segetum*
Field gladiolus

Cerinthe major
Honeywort

Tulipa boeotica
Found in central
Greece and the
Peloponnese

Allium roseum
Rose garlic

Nigella arvensis
A species of
love-in-the-mist

Psoralea bituminosa
Bitumen pea

*Lupinus
angustifolius*
Narrow-leaved
lupin

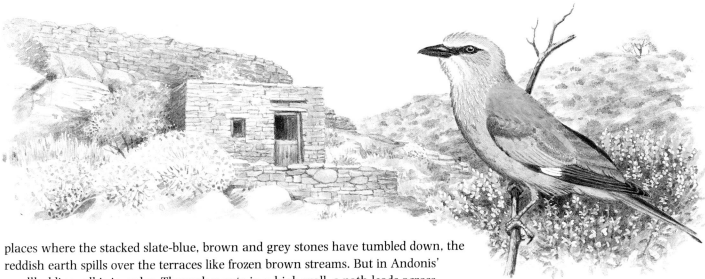

places where the stacked slate-blue, brown and grey stones have tumbled down, the reddish earth spills over the terraces like frozen brown streams. But in Andonis' smallholding, all is in order. Through a gate in a high wall, a path leads across rotavated olive terraces. The earth is humped for irrigation in exact rectangles around blocks of onions. Beyond a further gate, a pack of fiercely barking but tail-wagging dogs leads the way to a vine-shaded bower. Goldfish swim in a square reservoir, edged with whitewashed stone benches and slate pathways picked out with white. There is a Roman feeling about this haven of peace and quiet.

Below the monastery of Vrisis, where four monks still live, Peter paints the view down the ravine towards the village of Kastro, a white-cubed hump against the sea. The sun, at an angle over the steep hillside beyond the ravine, picks out the curving patterns of terrace walls with a decisive contrast between light and shade. The flat stones, laid on top of the walls, snake along like many-jointed trains. The olive trees ranged up the terraced slopes are black-trunked and ashen against the sun, like the embers of a wood fire. Below the courtyard of a little chapel there are massed lupins, the deepest blue. Their spires stand up in a delicate but military kind of way. Against the dazzle of the whitewashed church, they seem particularly Greek. Blue and white, the colours of the flag, are a typically Greek combination; blue sea and whitewashed stone typically Cycladean.

Further down the ravine, by a date palm with deep orange date seeds at its heart, its fanned, herringbone-striped leaves crisp in the sun, stands one of the island's many pigeon-houses. From its diamond and triangular-patterned openings, sprays of pigeons fly out at intervals like burnt paper blown in the wind, the white among them shining against the blue sky. There are far more pigeons tenanting the pigeon-houses than in the past. They say pigeons mean prosperity. On Sifnos the old proverb is proved.

The islands of the Cyclades provide good resting places for migratory birds. The beautiful blue and chestnut plumage of a roller, Coracias garrulus, *adds a further splash of colour to a terraced ravine bright with spring-flowering bushes: euphorbia, purple sage and yellow broom.*

Bee-eaters, Merops apiaster, *swoop after insects above a field thick with the daisies and poppies of cultivated land.*

September on Amorgos

The hill behind the grey square stones of the ruined tower is an indistinct mass as the sun, still below the horizon, rises unseen. A large herd of goats is moving slowly across the hillside, and their bells make a sound like bright water cascading over stones.

By half-past seven in the morning the eleven children have been gathered up from the scattered hamlets in the south of Amorgos, packed tightly into the island's single taxi, and driven to the high school in Hora, an hour away. The road, blasted out of rock not long ago, twists its stony, dusty way along the high backbone of the island, past peaks of jumbled rocks and slopes of dry earth sparsely covered in thistles and prickly bushes. On either side the land falls steeply to the sea. On the long south-east coast, the cliffs are sheer, forming a fortress wall, the final edge of the Cyclades before the stretch of sea that leads to the Dodecanese and the Turkish coast. To the north west, the island presents a less forbidding aspect, curving itself slightly like the palm of a welcoming hand and providing some shelter from the prevailing north wind that continually sends high seas crashing against its coast.

The wind is master of the islands. Gales can whip the sea to such heights that no boat can travel. There are times in winter when supplies run out: there is no paraffin, perhaps, or no sugar. We, who think we can make plans, organize our lives and our journeys to our own convenience and satisfaction, discover that we are as much at the mercy of the wind as thistledown, blown to seed itself wherever it may fall.

Islands appear on the horizon like figments of the imagination, pale dormant shapes. Pass an island by, and however close to its shores you come, its individual character cannot be guessed. One island looks much like another: a lump of brownish grey and ochre rising in various arrangements of peaks with splashes of white, a single church, a group of houses. There is little or no sign of movement; perhaps only a caique turning a promontory. Even the harbour will look dormant, more like a picture than reality. But set foot on the island, and it is as though a key has been turned. It seems that the island is resuming a life that was held in suspension until your arrival. And when you leave, and the figures on the quay shrink in the distance, a stillness comes over the scene again: it becomes once more a picture until your next visit.

On an island, there is a clear line between arrival and departure, between home and away. Costas, who has spent his life in the merchant navy, years away, months at home, is now at home. His wife Voula, who never left the island but brought up the four boys on her own, is now living in Athens so that the boys can study. Costas is doing odd painting jobs during his long leave. In Athens casual work like this is harder to find, he says. Vitsezos, who as a boy passed our house each day on his donkey, has returned to work on the island, after years in Athens as a carpenter and in Chicago as a cook. He has started a restaurant. Every family has its lines across the sea, its sons and daughters in Athens or abroad, its visiting relations.

And every island has its own character, its own atmosphere. It is not only the way an island lies in the sea, round and small, long and thin, jaggedly, smoothly, steeply or shallowly. It is not only the way it faces sun and wind, nor the way the main village is here perched high inland, or there low by the sea. The people of each island are as idiosyncratic to their island as natives to their country. This combination of natural and human characteristics exerts its influence on the visitors

The buzz and hum of high summer's insect life is so constant that it is scarcely heard; yet the insects themselves, with their intriguing behaviour patterns, are worth attention. The larva of the ant-lion (top) digs holes in sand to trap ants which it eats with its ferocious jaws. The female praying mantis (centre) is famed for her habit of eating the male after, and sometimes even during, mating. The female great green bush cricket (bottom) uses her external ovipositor to place her eggs in crevices. Only the males 'sing', by rubbing together their serrated wings.

an island attracts, and on the way an island develops in response to those visitors. One island will attract one kind of holidaymaker, those who want 'life' and music and dancing; another, those after quiet and solitude, harshness of landscape, simplicity. And each visitor will have a different experience of an island, finding in it what he has come to find – or if not, then leaving.

We each have pictures of a place and its people, and the reality, if such a thing can exist without a human viewpoint, is hard for us to grasp or understand. Has the islander who has never been away a greater understanding than the visitor who can make comparisons with other places, other people?

The sun, now high over the hills, bakes the broken threshing floor that lies between the ruined tower and the white chapel of Ayia Triadha. The goats have moved slowly across the threshing floor, tearing at the dry heads of last year's asphodel, followed by a 12-year-old girl and her older cousin. She has left school. As the youngest of the family, she must help at home. She has an elder brother studying in Athens. Has she ever been there? No. Would she like to go? Yes. Apart from an occasional trip to Hora, the furthest she has gone from her home is the hour by donkey over the hill and down to the beach in summer, and to the festival of Ayia Paraskevi, the church that overlooks the bay beyond.

From her house not far from the tower, her mother points out the path that leads between stone walls to Kato Kambo. This is the way we came from the sea some years ago with a friend, Martin Young, who was staying with us while working on a guide book to the Cyclades to follow his book on the Ionian islands. Then – it was October – the ground around the walls of Ayia Triadha was studded with golden yellow sternbergia. Now, in late September, there is no sign of the display that will appear in a few weeks' time. But partridges fly up with a clatter of wings and a chattering cry from the walls that edge the fields of stubble in a sheltered saddle of the hills, just as many and as raucously as on that earlier walk.

On the brow of the hill, where Sardinian warblers fly between thickets of lentisc and juniper, and crested larks rise in the air, there is a sudden glimpse of sea ahead. A little further on, the land falls away in a wide view. The islands of Karos, Antikeri and Grambousa are pinkish lumps sprawled to their necks in blue water and fringed with white froth.

On Grambousa, shearwaters gather for the night to roost. One night, camping on the beach, the silence of this small, uninhabited island was rent by sudden spine-chilling shrieks, the sound of babies being murdered. The family froze with horror for several minutes, until Peter suggested it was shearwaters. Old Kiria Maria, a granny to our children, was called the Grambousiani. Her family had lived there, and she too as a child: the last inhabitants.

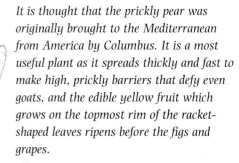

It is thought that the prickly pear was originally brought to the Mediterranean from America by Columbus. It is a most useful plant as it spreads thickly and fast to make high, prickly barriers that defy even goats, and the edible yellow fruit which grows on the topmost rim of the racket-shaped leaves ripens before the figs and grapes.

59

Between the rocky hills and the sea, the land spreads in a pattern of terraced fields. They lie around the scattered hamlets like the crocheted cloths on the tall, round side tables in Kiria Sofia's *saloni*. Yesterday Kiria Sofia gave us chocolate cake from Athens wrapped in silver paper, coffee, biscuits, sweets, a liqueur and, as she put it, 'something cool' – a bowl of trifle. A pair of portrait photographs, huge and gilt-framed, lean forward from high on the walls. The two fathers, Yannis' and Sofia's, look down with smiling and benevolent expressions, unusual in that period of grim-faced photographs. They would recognize the room's furnishings: chiffoniers with mirror shelves arranged with delicate bone china and engraved glass, little tables with china figurines sitting on crocheted cloths, solid high-backed chairs standing like soldiers at the central table and against the walls. A collage of silks and embroidery made by Sofia's aunt hangs in a frame. It shows Victory holding a laurel wreath over Greece and England to celebrate the end of the Second World War. Victory wears a red dress and silver wings and perches uncomfortably on something that looks like a goal-post. Greece is symbolized by an *Evzoni* in his guard uniform of white kilt, tights and pompommed boots, and England by a young man wearing long running shorts, dark blue ankle socks and neat white shoes with a single strap. He looks more likely to run a mile than fight a war. Later, Kiria Sofia came on board *Moby Dick* – a compliment of the highest order, for she feels seasick even in the harbour. When she visits her daughter and grandson in Athens, the journey is a nightmare.

Now, in the blue straits between the descending curves of the beige terraces and mottled grey-green hills of Amorgos and offshore Grambousa, a yacht struggles slowly against the sea. The wind is again force 7. The surface of the sea is torn into curling white shreds. The yacht rises, topples, falls, wallows, rises again, and rocks. In another hour it will have made the shelter of Katapola, where it will tie up alongside the other yachts; among them, the yacht of the couple who sold their house in Norway over three years ago and have been travelling ever since, across the Atlantic to the West Indies, and now to the Mediterranean.

'In the West Indies, the wind blows steadily and smoothly and always from the

The chapel of Ayia Triadha stands beside the well-preserved walls of an ancient Hellenic tower near Arkesini on Amorgos.

The view of the bay of Katapola, with the chapel of Ayios Pandeleimon on its promontory, was the backdrop to our life on the island.

60

same direction,' they say. 'You know exactly when you will arrive. Here, it's so unpredictable.' Yesterday they tried to leave, but turned back at the lighthouse. For them, Amorgos is a harbour with water and diesel available, in a difficult patch of sea that they will not re-visit. For Vitsezos, it is the place where he grew up, which he left to find work, and to which he can now return since the increase in visitors provides a livelihood. For the ravens and partridges and crested larks it is home. And for the birds that migrate between Africa and Europe it is as useful a resting and refuelling place as it is for the yachts and holidaymakers.

In the steep valley behind the bay of Katapola where the tiny church of Evangelismos sits like a dollop of meringue, bee-eaters flash in the sun, breaking their journey to Africa. Their colours are brilliant; sea-blue breasts, sun-yellow heads outlined in black, and soft orangey wings that are almost transparent in the air. They swoop and float and dive like Chinese kites, tails spread like those of fish, in pursuit of butterflies, insects, bees. Their calls are liquid – a fluting whistle that is sometimes shrill, and sometimes subdued as though piped beneath water.

Pandelis the fisherman orders bottle after bottle of beer, and talks of the helicopter

In September the vivid pink-and-white-speckled flowers of Colchicum variegatum *suddenly appear from the arid earth. The leaves which grow in the spring take nourishment down to the bulb to be stored for the following autumn's flowering.*

Increased spearfishing has severely reduced the number of fish in the rocky shallows. A grouper, the large fish in the centre, now hides in deeper water, as does the crayfish. The other fish shown here are still common: red mullet, with whiskers probing for food; parrot fish in two colour forms – grey and red, and all grey; four white bream and a solitary sheep's-head bream; tiny red cardinal fish; a brown long-snouted wrasse and a male and female rainbow wrasse.

61

Two fish of the open sea which sometimes visit coastal waters are the amberjack (top) and the pompona (below). The shining golden amberjack is usually solitary but the fork-tailed, silvery pompona is more often seen in small groups.

that brought people from Rhodes asking about seals. Pandelis has seen no seals at all for the last five years, but before that there used to be one every two or three miles in caves round the coast. Every year the fishing gets worse. The sea is overfished and he cites the usual reasons: better nets, more demand, more fishermen and more professional spearfishermen. There are those too who resort to dynamite, killing everything, the young fry and sometimes themselves into the bargain, as happened this year. It is no longer possible to catch what they call the May fish. The method was to drag white cloths in the water which attracted them. Pilot fish have similar habits; they swim along under flotsam. But the May fish no longer go after the cloths. The general opinion is that the fish nowadays follow all the white plastic bags which neither sink nor float but hang in the water, so the fishermen's cloths are no longer attractively unique. However, Pandelis still sees dolphins. They help herd pelamid into the nets. We remember the dolphin that was caught in his nets and drowned. He told us then that they would never eat dolphin because it is a friend of man, and quoted the story of Apollo. The strong taboo against killing dolphins is something young fishermen do not want to learn from their fathers.

Nor do the sons of shepherds wish to follow in their fathers' footsteps. On the brow of the hill above the house where we used to live, Yorgos' house is empty. The island stretches away to the south west, the wedge shape of Mount Korakas beginning the final descent of hills to the southernmost cape of Grambousa island like the first clear letter of an illegible signature. Waves break in white spray down the length of the coast. The church of Ayios Pandeleimon sits on its promontory, a firm landmark underlining the familiarity of the view. Thistles, dry sticks of asphodel, wire-netting bushes crowd between the stones of the threshing floor. Bushes of prickly pear in front of the house grow thick and unchecked over the walls. Yet there are signs that goats are still sometimes penned in the collapsing stone sheds and graze the terraces below where colchicum is flowering. From the dry earth, even before the first autumn rains, almost stemless crocus-shaped flowers open their six blotched purple petals. The leaves grow later, in the winter rains after the flowers have shrivelled, and take nourishment down to the bulbs so that next year they can flower again.

It is hard to imagine life returning to the ruined cottages of island shepherds. That high hillside life is unlikely to flower again.

Fishermen look on the dolphin as the friend of man and quote the story of how Apollo was brought to Delphi on a dolphin's back. But dolphins sometimes damage nets and take the fish – and not all young fishermen share their elders' belief that killing a dolphin brings bad luck.

Central Greece

Athens sits in the centre of Greece like a spider in its web. It is the beginning and end of journeys. There are not many capital cities so well placed. Delphi in its time was regarded as the centre not only of Greece but of the whole world. Yet both Athens and Delphi are well to the south of the region generally called Central Greece.

The title of this chapter refers to the central chunk of the mainland, an area as diverse as Greece itself. Groups of islands fall neatly into chapters. The Peloponnese has a distinct character of its own. So does north-eastern Greece. It is easy enough to take a knife to the country and divide it into areas which have strong local identities. But the central part that is left when the edges have been trimmed is an area so varied that it is impossible to summon an identifying image.

The southern Pindos chain of mountains, running north–south, forms a massive barrier between west and east. The mountain of Parnassos continues the line which ends with the three mountains that form the armchair facing the sea in which Athens sprawls – Parnis, Pendelis and Hymettos. Another long line of mountains, an offshoot from the northern Pindos, runs down the eastern coast: Pieria and then Olympos, the giant of the Greek mountains, followed by Kissavos, Ossa, Pilion, Othrys and the mountains of the offshore island of Evvia. These complex ranges are worlds of their own. Each provides a habitat for an immense variety of wildlife: plants, insects, reptiles, birds, butterflies and mammals, all interdependent. The mountains turn the plains and plateaux between them into islands too, with individual characteristics. The low-lying marshes and cypress-studded hills of the western coast are very different from the vast fertile expanse of the plain of Thessaly and the orchards of Pilion in the east. On Olympos grow flowers that are found nowhere else. There are otters living in the irrigation ditches of the plains. Hares, stone martens and foxes are a usual enough sight in all the mountains of the region, but wolves, wild boar and bears are confined to the wildest reaches of the Pindos. One image common to all the plains of mainland Greece is a stork sitting on its unwieldy nest of branches balanced against all odds on the top of a telegraph pole.

The hatchet-faced mountain of Tsouka, 1795 metres high, is one of the many peaks that make up the complicated mountain ranges of the southern Pindos. The villages of Stournareïka, Elati and Pertouli are ringed by three of these: the mountains of Avgo, Koziakis and Karavoula. The fir forests of this region of high peaks and deep gorges give shelter to much wildlife.

Opposite: the river Pinios which rises in the central Pindos enters the plain of Thessaly at Kalambaka. In the fourteenth century isolated pinnacles of smooth rock beyond the town provided natural refuges for religious hermits, who built monasteries on the peaks. This is Meteora, where Egyptian vultures gather in great numbers, circling the plains and the pinnacles for prey. Alpine swifts flicker in the dark chasms below, lit by the sun like dust motes.

Athens

After a day up in the mountains, the last stretch of the road back to Athens held a unique quality. It was getting dark as the road descended gently in a straight line that never seemed to end. The four friends in the car were dazed by fresh air, new places, and in the dark travelling box they began to sing. Every Greek song Nikos and Oliga knew was sung and sung and sung, and learnt by us without effort. By the time the lights of Athens appeared, spangling the seat of its mountain armchair before the sea, songs were being retrieved from childhood. Theodorakis gave way to raucous playground chants. Passing the outlying suburbs of Kifissia and Psychiko, a husband was going to the market to buy his wife a cock that would shout 'ki-ki-ri-ki-ki' to wake her up in the morning. Skimming past the Zappion park and into Syntagma Square, a whole chain of noisy animals would be promised from the market: woofing dogs, miaowing cats, mooing cows, hee-hawing donkeys.

In those days, there were few cars on the road. Nikos and Oliga, like the great majority of Athenians, had no transport of their own. Greece, outside Athens, was a strange country to them. They shared many of our first explorations. With Yannis and Vasso we learnt the names of the fish that moved between the rocks off the coast of Attica. With another Yannis, Peter spent a day among the butterflies and flowers of Parnassos. On the slopes of Mount Parnis, he sketched Cleopatra brimstones and dawn-clouded yellow butterflies.

Athena, the goddess of wisdom, was first worshipped on the Acropolis in the Middle Helladic period, about 1500 BC, when the settlement around its slopes became a town bearing her name. The little owl depicted on this ancient 4-drachma coin was the symbol of the goddess and is still the symbol of the city and of wisdom.

Now, on a smart hotel roof in the centre of Athens, there is a swimming-pool and a marble-clad bar. Pollution has eaten into the veins of the marble. Parnis is all but invisible. There is merely a hint that the city is bounded on three sides by the humps of Parnis, Pentelis and Hymettos and gives way on its fourth side to the sea. Flat-topped blocks prickled over with wires and aerials fade away on all sides in a series of pale mushroom shades. The Acropolis, the Parthenon now fenced off, stands on its rocky table on one side, and the pinnacle of Lykavitos rises out of steep streets on the other. Despite strong measures to control traffic – a ban on cars with even number licence plates one day, odd numbers the next – there is a jam the length of Panepistimiou street. A trolley bus has become derailed at Omonia Square, and behind it a chain of trolleys stretches back to Syntagma. They look like the yellow and black caterpillars that come down from the pines in winter and amble in long trails across the pavements of Psychiko, the suburb where a manufacturer's three daughters once read Enid Blyton with their English teacher.

North of Psychiko is the wooded suburb of Kifissia. Gracious old houses stand in green and shaded gardens. Here Niki Goulandris, daughter of the shipping magnate, has created a Natural History Museum. In cool marble halls, golden eagles and lammergeier stand motionless for study; Hermann's tortoise can be differentiated from the spur-thighed tortoise; the symbol of an oil company identified as the shell *Proteus glaber*. There is a herbarium where the wild flowers of Greece are studied and painted. All is well ordered and meticulous.

There are others too who care deeply for the wildlife of Greece. In the offices of the Hellenic Society for the Protection of Nature, Byron Antipas is sprightly and smiling, constantly fetching files thick with cuttings, evidence of immense battles over the

Acanthus spinosus grows beside the stone acanthus of a fallen column. Sculptors in ancient Greece frequently used natural forms as the basis of patterns in their work.

The shapes of flowers and leaves were formalized to make repetitive designs as on this capital by the Parthenon. The stylized palm-leaf pattern is called a palmette.

years. His assistant, Peter Broussalis, seems more cast down by these battles. He sighs over his map of red, green and yellow spots. The spots indicate areas designated in three ways: as National Parks, Aesthetic Forests and Monuments of Nature. It seems that these grand titles mean very little in practice. The bulletin *Nature*, which the Society produces when it can, contains hope; not in its tales of destruction and extinction but in its evidence that there is a growing number of people who are studying, reporting, and campaigning on behalf of Greek wildlife.

A notice on the gate leading to the site of Athens' ancient market pleads on behalf of striking museum guards: 'Please assist the rights of the workers.' How this should be done is not clear. The strikers have locked the gate; so perhaps one should simply assist the strike by not rattling its chain, or climbing over. A visit to the Agora has always been an essential part of time spent in Athens. On one side of the gate is modern Athens, with all the headaches of city life, the pandemonium of too much traffic, too many people trying to do different things, the tourist market and the junk market; and, on the other, the old market in a hollow beneath the Acropolis. It was in the Agora that we first became enthused by the possibility of a book on Greek landscape and wildlife.

'Delicious air, smells, sights,' an old notebook says. 'Blossom, yellow jasmine, white almond, pink cherry; Judas trees brilliantly milky-purple. Man-made grottiness next door to man-made perfection – the proportions of the temple of Ephaistos, dark upright oblong, framing sunlit view of Acropolis like a keyhole. Mellow stone. Man's eccentricity, too – groups of tourists arouse curiosity, amazement and wonder as much as plants, architecture, history. Everything seems for a moment intensely weird and wonderful. Such strange sights – man in breeches and green stockings. Another, grey-bearded, short and stocky, in woolly cap, patterned sweater, brown shorts, white legs, woollen socks – the whole thing festooned with camera straps and striding along beside a bigger wife, a nightmarish Brunhilde. They cross the mid-distance at a cracking pace. Brunhilde turns and gives me a ghastly look when she feels my stare on the little husband at her side. Parties with guides – the mesmerized expressions, caged looks, and the monotone of the guide, as unrelenting and unswitch-offable as the hotel's too modern shower. In the museum, heightened perception still in action, almost painfully: the economy, sureness and rightness of line. Wanted to somehow trap this feeling (in the way some people need to photograph), so I copied the profile of a woman from an amphora – eye, nose, mouth, chin. The label below told me: the transverse line at the mouth indicated the archaic smile, *c.*810 BC. I felt I must be wearing an archaic smile too.'

This book had begun.

Delphi and Parnassos

In the town of Delphi, an elderly widow talks of her husband. He had worked most of his life on the ancient site with a famous archaeologist. He always said that Delphi was the centre of the world in ancient times, and the most beautiful place in the world today. She thinks this must be true, because people come here from all over the world at all times of the year. Her husband had been very learned. Although he had not been born in Delphi, he had never wanted to live anywhere else. She herself had been local, an ordinary local girl, she says.

Around a curve of the mountainside and under the shade of olive trees below the Sacred Precinct, a party of workmen from the further village of Arachova is clearing a rockfall. They offer a drink of cold water from their pitcher and talk of football. Higher up, parties of schoolchildren have reached the Stadium. Applause breaks in waves, great salvos of cheers rise into the blue air as another circuit is completed. One lad has run the 600 Roman-foot track 25 times.

By the Treasury of the Sifnians, built with the gold-mining profits of the island of Sifnos, a guide informs her audience that this was 'the first time in the history of architecture that girls were used in place of columns'. This startling information is repeated in French, Italian and German. The faces of her audience stare glumly at the stones. It is hard to tell what is in their minds: the image of real girls holding up the Treasury's roof? Admiration of the 6th century BC sculptural innovation? Or are they wishing they had worn different shoes, or regretting their previous evening's decision to try the stuffed vine leaves?

While the coaches line up on the road below the site and brightly coloured parties wind their way through the ruins, the natural life of the place goes on. A blue rock thrush builds its nest. A swallowtail butterfly emerges from its chrysalis. The colours of the flowers which now, in spring, trail in profusion among the ruins are mainly yellow and purple. *Campanula rupestris*, honesty, convolvulus and grape hyacinth make up the range of purples, mauves and blues. Besides the common but pretty yellow-flowered *Bunias erucago* there are bushes of greeny-yellow euphorbia, the drooping yellow trumpets of onosma and the golden lace caps of *Smyrnium perfoliatum*. Higher up the slopes, yellow asphodel is just starting to flower, and, in among the rocks, various orchids and *Iris pumila attica* add deeper colours to the scene.

The wild flowers of spring crowd a terrace above the three remaining pillars of the circular Tholos at Delphi. Among umbellifers, vetches, red anemones and Bermuda buttercup grow pale lilac Knautia integrifolia, *the yellow and red-tinged pendants of* Onosma graeca, Smyrnium perfoliatum *and* Muscari comosum.

From this height above Delphi, it is easier to feel the magic of the place, a magic which cannot be erased no matter how many of us trudge, hot and tired, up and down its paths. The massive rocks that rise in a semi-circle above accentuate the feeling that this is indeed the navel of the earth. Below, the few remaining honey-coloured pillars of the Temple of Apollo stand etched against the blue-grey fuzz of olives that descend steeply way way down to the valley of the river Pleistos. From the hidden ravine, Mount Kivrys rises steeply in the distance, as though protecting Delphi from the sea. To the west, olive groves sweep, like the sea itself, down to the plain of Itea and its harbour.

Below the road and the three patched pillars of the Tholos, a track zigzags down through the olives. Immediately the queues of coaches and noises of the road are forgotten. It is a timeless pastoral scene. The terraces are smothered in flowers, clumps of golden and purple honeywort, yellow alkana, white umbellifers, scarlet poppies. Two bees lumber drowsily in the silken red head of a poppy. There is a slow, busy rustling in a small lentisc bush. The noise continues, twigs stir this way and that, then a tortoise appears. Its shell looks like an apple pie, its edges pressed into a pattern by a thumb. It regards the sky with an ages-old eye.

Two men are gathering olives. One is up a tree, beating the branches with a stick. The other, an older man, is picking up the olives. While he has a moment's help, he talks of the water conduit which now blazes across the landscape, underlining Delphi. It comes from the mountains above Nafpaktos, he says, and takes water to Athens, a 1 in 100 decline. Athens needs so much water nowadays, he explains, because everyone has baths; not like in the old days when one just needed a little to splash on one's face and hands.

At the bottom of the ravine a bridge crosses the river Pleistos which flows milky-green over white stones. On the far side, craggy rocks rise one above the other, as though trying to see above the silver-leaved olives that crowd the steep hillside. But the view of Delphi is clear even from this distance. Far above, the sheltering arms of the Phaedriades, the Shining Rocks like pumpkins lit from within, cradle the ancient site. The columns and the seats in the amphitheatre appear neatly etched. Here and there, Judas trees blaze against the blue-green background. Some are so laden with milky-purple blossom that the branches are scarcely visible. The colour is resounding. Everything appears so clear and intense, it seems to have a sound of its own. The sky, untouched azure, is a further distant sound – an oboe, perhaps. The crags make organ music, scales and chords in *crescendo*. The olives, with their silver-sided leaves noticing a breeze that nothing else can feel, are plucked harps. Judas blossom is strident, a clarinet or a trumpet.

Snow still lies on the highest slopes of Parnassos in April but a flat meadow where the snow has melted is a lake of blue Scilla bifolia *and* Crocus veluchensis.

The two colour forms, purple and yellow, of Iris pumila attica *grow side by side below the fir trees of Parnassos.*

One female and two male siskins, Carduelis spinus, *perch on a branch of Greek fir,* Abies cephalonica. *The siskin is a common bird of fir forests and mixed woodlands. Its streaked greenish-yellow plumage makes it similar to the serin and greenfinch, but it is smaller than the greenfinch and its characteristic yellow wing-bars differentiate it from both. Serins and greenfinches prefer more open habitats.*

Golden eagles once hung in the chasms above Delphi. The oliver-gatherers say that the shepherds of Parnassos have shot them all. Their place has been taken by Alpine choughs and gulls. A mass of gulls, white and screeching, disappears over the rocky skyline. From here it seems that this line must be the earth's limit. Beyond, there can be nothing but blue.

Perhaps invaders thought the same. The people of Delphi, in times of danger, would simply climb steps cut in the rock above, and disappear into the blue. The unsettling thought that the next world began at the skyline, or simply the punishing climb, deterred pursuit. The enemy would move on. The people of Delphi would emerge from their hiding place, the huge Corcyrian cave, and return to their homes below the skyline.

Looking down from the platform at the entrance to the cave, this jagged rim has become a tame, faintly-green undulation clad with patches of fir, a simple boundary to a flat plain and the first of a series of similar lines that recedes southwards towards the distant peaks of the Peloponnese. There is no sense that the earth beyond this first boundary falls away in the precipices of Delphi. This is a different world. The plain below the platform is cultivated in strips and patches. There are hummocks of firs and rocks, and a murky, motionless patch of brown water where the gulls are gathering. The cave is huge and dank, hung with stalactites. Its modern name is Sarantavli. 'Forty Rooms'. Its hollowness echoes; room enough in here to hide several villages.

There is still snow lying on the peaks of Parnassos, which rise from the northeastern side of the plain, and one or two cars, with skis strapped to roofracks, show that the ski-ing season is not yet over. In the fir-clad foothills, fences mark building plots and there is a straggle of newly built houses. Some look as though they have been designed by Hansel and Gretel's architect. Town-dwellers used to look down on the country as a place they had escaped from, a place where their poor relations lived. Now they value it as a place to escape to, from the smoggy city. A weekend retreat in the country is the present dream. There is a new law against building in National Forest, but it is questionable how much of the Parnassian forest can remain as it is.

None the less, it is still an immensely empty place. Anemone *blanda* lie in blue pools at the foot of tall black firs. Every so often the firs give way to sheltered rocky hollows where the ground is a lacy mat of speedwell, forget-me-not, yellow ragwort, sedum, shepherd's purse, vetches, lousewort, grape hyacinth, campion, euphorbia. In the centre of a high, stony plain there is something metallic blue shining. Is this a pool of melted snow, or perhaps a powder, a mineral deposit? It lies where a lake might lie in such a place. As we draw nearer, the puzzle is solved. The plain is flooded with palest purple crocus and bright blue scilla. It is impossible to walk without crushing the flowers underfoot. The snow has not long melted. But it has dried so quickly in the hot sun that it has cracked into miniature crazy paving. Here and there, the shoot of a crocus has lifted one piece of crazy paving, which now sits at a slant on the tip of the shoot. The weight of that small triangle of dried earth demonstrates the strength of the flower beneath.

Peter is now painting a view of Parnassos. A lizard's head emerges from a crack in a fallen tree beside him. It is a thin slick of a thing, its perfect splayed feet gripping the edge of the crack. It decides it is safe to come out completely, and it slips jerkily over the barkless, shining oyster-pink log. A buzzard floats overhead like a paper kite, the centre of each wing letting through the sun like parchment. Little siskins dip and dive from fir to fir, flashing pale green-yellow in the sun. Their song is such a tiny twittering; it sounds like a distant sizzling frying-pan, suggests Peter. There is a raven croaking, a very black high-up sound, and a great tit insistently peeps – the peep, peep, peep of an unanswered telephone. There is a mass of *Anemone blanda*, in colours varying from blue to lilac to white, with pale yellow centres, the bright yellow shining stars of gagea, and pure white ornithogalum, Star of Bethlehem. Yellow and purple iris flower among the white rocks of the hillside. A blue butterfly pirouettes on a tiny pink flower. Other butterflies, fritillaries, small coppers, two sorts of brimstone, painted ladies, various whites, skim over the rocks. How can snow still lie deep on Parnassos in the background of the picture when there is such intense sun, life and colour in the foreground?

And is it possible that just over the rim of the plain and only a few kilometres below, there is that other world of coaches and guides, and Delphi?

A Hermann's tortoise, Testudo hermanni, *emerges from the undergrowth. Unlike other tortoises in Greece it has not one but two plates above the tail and a large scale on the tail's tip.*

A pair of golden eagles, Aquila chrysaetos, *guard their single chick on a high crag. The numbers of these once-common eagles are declining. They are shot by shepherds and hunters and poisoned by pesticides transmitted in the food chain.*

Evvia and Pilion

Day after day during the long summer months, the sun rises on one horizon, draws a slow arc across the blue dome of sky and sinks on the other. Though there will be days that are hotter or cooler than others, days when the wind is stronger and from a different quarter, days when a few scattered clouds will bank over the sun, even the occasional day of storm or sudden rain, that steady progress of the sun across the sky is always evident. It gives a dependable and visible rhythm to the days, and country people live closely in tune with it. It is interesting to wonder how much the position of a village influences the general personality of the villagers. Do people who live on slopes that are lit by the sun early in the morning have a more optimistic view of life? Are they more energetic than those living on slopes facing west, who receive the sun later in the morning? Does the constant sight of a setting sun, particularly if it sets in the sea, induce a nostalgic frame of mind – a fondness for the past, rather than optimism for the future? If people have a choice in the matter, does that choice reflect their natural disposition?

Streams in dry areas attract many insects. Drinking from a stream on Evvia are green hairstreaks, Callophrys rubi, *and a southern white admiral,* Limenitis reducta.

Stone martens, also known as beech martens, Martes foina, *are common in most areas of Greece although, being nocturnal, they are seldom seen. They have a whiter bib than the similar pine martens of Northern Europe. There are no stoats in Greece but many weasels,* Mustela nivalis. *The male weasel, twice the size of the female, is about half the size of a stone marten, whose body can be as much as half a metre long.*

On the eastern shores of Evvia hillsides green with pines descend steeply to the sea. In spring tree heather, Erica arborea, *rock roses, Judas trees and terebinth flower among craggy white rocks above coves of clear green water. Such places, remote from roads and villages, provide safe habitats for wild life.*

Nikos chose a headland on the eastern coast of Evvia. Today even the Delphian widow's husband might have agreed that this, not Delphi, is the most beautiful place on earth. It is the second week in April. The sun is hot, the sea like glass. There is the faintest little breath of cooling air every so often, and birdsong is the only sound.

The tent stands under a wood and canvas shelter on a saddle of flattened cleared earth between two rocky humps. Pines, tree heather, olives, Judas trees, lentisc, arbutus, myrtle and daphne grow between jagged white boulders which descend steeply to the sea. On each side of this private peninsula lies a curve of beige sand.

There is a single event. A shepherd called Yorgos comes down through the pines from a high village with his herd of glossy goats. While he talks with Nikos, the goats, mostly black but a few with reddish-brown tinges, take the chance to lie in the sand, lick themselves and roll like dogs. A few try the sea as a drink. At the far end of the beach, sweet stream water flows fast down the hillside between plane trees. A short distance up the hill, the cold, clear waters of a spring join the stream. Here, green hairstreak butterflies drink and water bottles are filled.

At night, stone martens emerge from their holes in the hillsides to hunt. Nikos describes how one day he watched a fluffy-tailed marten cross the beach and enter the sea. It swam the length of the bay and climbed out, wet-furred, half the size.

There are stories too of long court cases, and villagers with guns. Peter, while sketching, keeps finding tools that have been missing; tins of food, bashed but unopened; scattered sugar; a rusty camp stove. Behind the beauty of the scene, there is a current of village resentment. Had Nikos the right to fence the land? Did the man who sold Nikos the land own the whole area now fenced? But the legal battle of ownership and boundaries is simply the focus of less tangible emotions. The road from Halkis, the island's main town, has only recently reached the villages above this stretch of eastern coast. Before this, the villagers' sole contact with the outside world was the occasional caique, or the long cross-country journey by mule or donkey. Small communities like this throughout Greece, often with piratical

Hooded crows mob a heron as it flies across a cove on Evvia. Corvus corone cornix, *with grey and black plumage, is a sub-species of the black* Corvus corone corone, *the carrion crow of northern Europe.*

A sand boa, Eryx jaculus, *lies coiled in the dappled shade of plane trees behind a sandy beach. This is a stout snake up to 80 cm long that feeds on small rodents, often constricting them before swallowing. It is the only constricting boa in Europe.*

traditions and the problems of inbreeding, are suffering from culture shock. Any newcomer, Greek or foreigner, will buy with his country retreat layer upon layer of social history. In the first heady celebration of owning this perfect headland miles from anywhere, Nikos and Polly plunged naked into the blue water of the deserted cove. However sensitive and aware the swimmer, who was to imagine that somewhere in the empty landscape there was a pair of eyes? But instantly they became not just rich Athenians who are always on holiday and who do not know what a day's work means but, far worse, an immoral and dangerous influence.

As the dark shadows of the hills behind lengthen over the sand, a heron crosses the bay, pursued and mobbed by hooded crows. They are defending their territory.

Evvia, the largest island after Crete, lies close to the eastern shores of the mainland and in a similar long slant from north-west to south-east. Its north-western point is separated from the bulge of the mainland's Mount Othrys by a narrow channel and the southern tip of the Pilion peninsula curls towards it, all but turning the bay of Volos, the Pegassitikos Gulf, into an inland lake. In its turn, the Pilion peninsula echoes the slant and shape of Evvia. Like Evvia, it is thickly wooded, with steep cliffs on its eastern shores and gentler slopes facing the west and the mainland. But the far smaller scale of the Pilion peninsula gives it a special beauty.

Travelling round Pilion has something of the flavour of a fairground ride. Tortuous roads lead from one view to another: from lush green orchards to heathy hills, from villages by the enclosed waters of the western coast to high villages with long views over the windswept Aegean. In the south, the rounded hills are so thick with vegetation that from a distance they look like efficient and bristling doormats. The bracken is tinged russet, the blue flowers of chicory are like fallen pieces of sky. The pale white flowers of clematis sprawl in profusion over ripening blackberries, thyme is flowering pale lilac, the dried seedheads of rock rose are mauve-grey. After the night's thunderstorm, there is an intoxicating herb smell from the hillsides. Hoopoes fly low between round-headed pines.

From Siki, a village where stray visitors are regarded with the utmost surprise, tracks lead down the rough hillside to two shingle beaches. The further beach is reached through a narrow green gorge where Peter sits painting. He is dive-bombed by huge fat flies, hornets and wasps. There is nothing to fear from the hornets and wasps because they will only sting in self-defence. But the flies belong to the various species of Tabanidae. They are horse flies and depend on warm blood for their sustenance. They are like mosquitoes, in that only the female bites. The males feed on nectar. Unfortunately, it is impossible to tell whether the encroaching dive-bomber is male or female; but at least its approach is audible. Far worse are the cleg flies. These are completely silent. A sudden sharp pain is the first intimation of a visit. Like a heavy-handed vaccinator, it can produce instant anger. The sight of prone sunbathers shooting upright and slapping themselves with furious shrieks is a sure sign that clegs are about.

Although it is August, these two beaches are deserted. It is the north-eastern part of Pilion that attracts the holiday-makers. What a relief it must be to come here from hot dusty towns and scorching plains. The precipitous slopes of Mount Pilion are thickly covered in beech and chestnut woods. Clear streams rush down rocky gullies. Villages of square stone houses with fishscale roofs of overlapping slates are stacked on ledges on the mountainside, as though on staircase landings. Water spills from fountains in plane-treed squares. The air is bright and brisk. Far below, the open sea sparkles and waves curl into foam on hidden beaches.

A man is scything long grass and bracken in an apple orchard. Fruit-crates and chestnut timbers are stacked on roadside verges. On Pilion there is a feeling of abundance, a heady luxury. The peninsula provides not only shade and water in plenty, but fruit, nuts, timber and attar of roses.

Thistles and vetch high on Mount Pilion attract various insects. At the top of the picture is a humming-bird hawk-moth, Macroglossum stellatarum. *Below is a hornet,* Vespa crabro, *and on the far left a robber fly,* Machimus atricapillus, *lies in wait for its prey – another insect. In the foreground is a potter wasp, genus* Eumenes, *one of the many wasps of Greece. The female mixes sand with her saliva to make a pot-shaped nest for her eggs.*

RARE FLOWERS OF THE WOODS AND MOUNTAINS

However great the temptation wild flowers must never be picked, particularly those as rare and spectacular as these. Their numbers are declining.

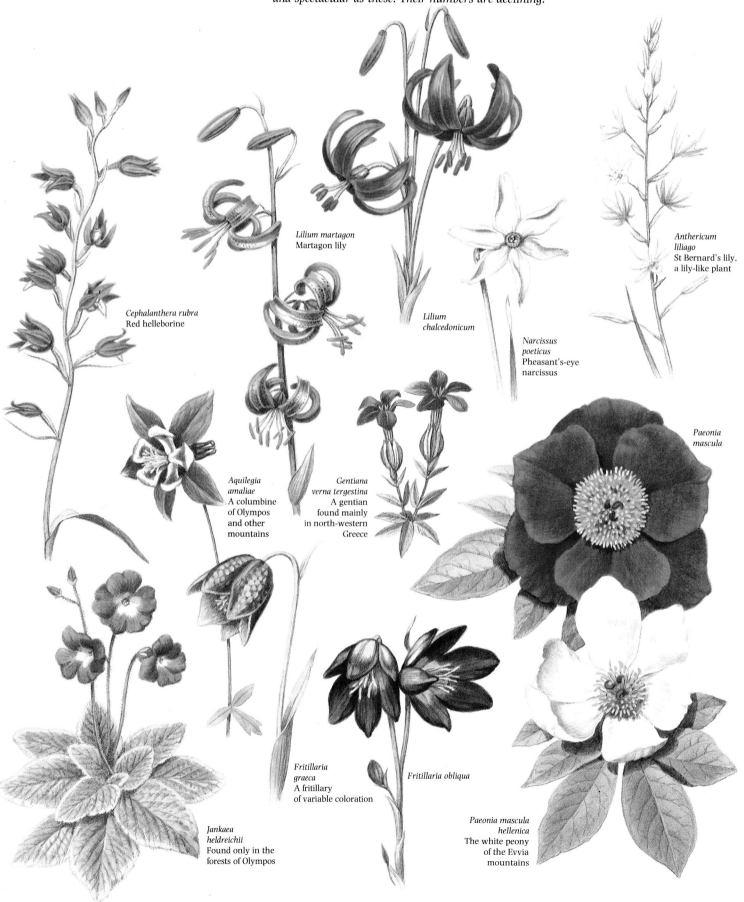

Lilium martagon
Martagon lily

Cephalanthera rubra
Red helleborine

Lilium chalcedonicum

Narcissus poeticus
Pheasant's-eye narcissus

Anthericum liliago
St Bernard's lily, a lily-like plant

Aquilegia amaliae
A columbine of Olympos and other mountains

Gentiana verna tergestina
A gentian found mainly in north-western Greece

Paeonia mascula

Jankaea heldreichii
Found only in the forests of Olympos

Fritillaria graeca
A fritillary of variable coloration

Fritillaria obliqua

Paeonia mascula hellenica
The white peony of the Evvia mountains

The Castle of Platamona and Mount Olympos

The massive range of Mount Olympos forms the eastern end of the mountain barrier that stretches across the mainland. The only easy way from north to south is confined to the narrow neck of land where the long slopes of its foothills almost reach the sea. Here the Castle of Platamona was built in the early thirteenth century by the Crusaders. It watched over the entrance to the Thermaic Gulf, the sea road to Thessaloniki, and guarded the way south.

On Easter Day mules graze on the daisy-covered meadows below the castle walls. A nightingale sings in a thicket of pomegranate and kermes oak. There are sprays of fluffy berry-like flowers on the oak, and the new leaves of the pomegranate are russet in the sun. The colours of newly-emerged butterflies – speckled woods and painted ladies – are vivid against the flowers: purple anemones, orange marigolds, blue anchusa. Clumps of golden alyssum grow in the ochre walls, and in the background the snow-rounded dome of Mount Olympos stands distant and aloof.

The Olympos massif is the highest of all Greek mountains. Mytikas, its summit, is 2,917 metres above the sea, which lies no more than 10 or 15 kilometres to the east. Not only is Olympos the mountain nearest to the sky, but its many peaks are awesome in their size and splendour. Nowhere else could be such a fitting home for the rumbustious, unpredictable and frightening family of ancient Greek gods. The landscape is built for them. Round a chasm, 450 metres deep, four peaks sit in a semi-circle. One of these peaks, armchair-shaped, is called the Throne of Zeus, and the chasm is called the Cauldrons. It is easy to imagine Zeus, sprawled in his armchair, tipping with his foot into the depths of the mist-filled cauldron any overbold mortal who had dared stray this far.

In August, Peter sits painting by a stream that cascades over huge boulders. Grey-streaked pinky-beige and corruscated cliffs rise among pine, beech and fir trees into clouds hanging wetly over the heights. A dark fawn and speckled frog crouches akimbo on a boulder over a clear pool. Downstream, a goatherd scalds milk over a fire. Cheeses drain in tins hungs from the branches of firs. The bells of the goats ring as they move over the steep tree-clad slopes. Wood warblers sing above the stream. In the undergrowth, there is a tall lilac-pink orchid still flowering so late in the year. There are cyclamen and wild strawberries, the yellow flowers of hypericum, tiny white-flowered box, and hummocks of feathery arching grasses and pink crane's bill.

Olympos is a world of its own. A whole book has been written on its flowers alone. Many of them are endemic, like the *Jankaea heldreichii* that is growing from a tight rosette of leaves at the foot of a beech tree by the stream. It looks a little like a primula, but its flowers are pinky-lavender and bell-shaped. Higher, there are lammergeier vultures soaring above the peaks. One is said to make a habit of visiting a mountain refuge hut where the caretaker gives it scraps of food.

Squatting on the dark grey rock of a stream on Mount Olympos a stream frog, Rana graeca, *is almost invisible.*

Above: on a hot August day clouds hide the peaks of Olympos and tall firs give welcome shade.

In spring a Cretzschmar's bunting, Emberiza caesia, *perches on a rock below the Castle of Platamona. Snow can still be seen on Mount Olympos in the distance.*

Through the Vale of Tempe and across the plains

Shrikes like to perch, usually alone, on telegraph wires watching for prey: insects, small birds and rodents which they impale on thorns to eat later. On the left: a lesser grey shrike, Lanius minor. Centre: a woodchat shrike, Lanius senator. Right: a male and a juvenile (with barred breast) red-backed shrike, Lanius collurio.

The cupolas of churches, roofs and telegraph poles are popular nesting sites for storks. It is thought that they bring good luck.

Below Olympos, the way south is forced through a narrow gorge, the Vale of Tempe. At the base of rugged russet and grey cliffs, a river rushes eastwards to the sea. This is the Pinios, which rises far to the west in the Pindos mountains and flows across the vast plain of Thessaly to meet the barrier formed by the mountains of Olympos and Ossa. In the Quarternary Epoch, this barrier was split and the water which had formed the Larissan Lake suddenly found an exit to the sea. This epoch covers the period from two million years ago, the time of the Ice Ages, to the emergence of man, and it is fascinating to think this gigantic upheaval might have been witnessed. Herodotus, writing in the 5th century BC, reported that the people of Thessaly believed that Poseidon, the god of the sea, had caused the upheaval. As soon as man learnt the art of communication, stories were passed down the generations. Perhaps, like the story of Poseidon's creation of the Vale of Tempe, every legend has grown from a real event.

Tempe is full of legends. Apollo washed himself in the river after he had killed the serpent Python. Then he cut a sprig of sweet bay which he planted by the Castalian Fountain in his sanctuary at Delphi. Certainly *Laurus nobilis* still grows along the banks of the river, overhung with plane trees and willows. In spring, the blossom of Judas trees makes bright splashes of purple against the dark cliffs.

To the south rises the mountain of Ossa. Between its lower slopes and the sea stretches a beach some 10 kilometres long, backed by orchards and a straggle of little holiday houses, the beginnings of development. At night, tree frogs make an orchestra of liquid sound in the undergrowth. From Ayiokambos a pretty road winds inland over the foothills of Ossa to the Dossion plain where once the pent-up waters of the Pinios formed the lake of Larissa. Now it is a flat and fertile expanse. There are fields of sugar beet, potatoes, ochre patches of corn stubble, almond orchards. Irrigation pipes send twisting Vs of water circling over the crops, the sun lighting rainbows in the spray. In the far distance there are low, scrubby hills. The division between plain and hills is so abrupt, it is as though the hills have been added later and are unconnected. Dust could collect in the crease, as under a skirting board.

In this beige and ochre landscape, there is food in plenty for numberless birds. There are nine lesser kestrels perching on the crossbars of a single telephone pole. They alight with a sweep of wings, dipping their spatulate tails two or three times as they settle down. The sun lights their speckled tawny breasts. They are as fat and watchful as cats. One has a chunk of pinkish meat in its claw which it brings forward and bends over to tear at with its curved beak, like an ill-mannered diner scooping food into his mouth. Goldfinches peck at the purple heads of thistles. Rollers, bee-eaters and shrikes – the lesser grey, the red-backed and the woodchat shrike – skim over the waving heads of reeds that edge the fields. Storks pick their way fastidiously over patches of ploughed earth.

Plains such as this and the great Plain of Thessaly, which at first sight seem flat and featureless, are full of life. They are habitats for wildlife which have been made richer by man's agricultural progress. Boys once herded flocks of turkeys over the stony scrub of the hillsides beyond the plain. Now irrigation and machinery have changed the landscape. Good red earth has been cleared of stones and rocks; crops have been planted. The false acacia trees which were planted along the verges when the main road was made are now big enough for birds to nest in. Sparrows' nests are like weaver birds' nests – little tunnelled cocoons hanging from the branches. Crested larks, swifts, martins and swallows are all attracted by roads: there is a mass of insects in the warm currents of air created by traffic. Magpies, which also nest in the roadside trees, scavenge for food, finding it in litter and the flattened corpses of rabbits, tortoises and hares. In some parts of the Plain of Thessaly, there are otters living along river banks where willows and undergrowth provide enough cover. Irrigation ditches also make good homes for otters, as long as the thick margin of reed and vegetation is not cut too frequently or, far worse, chemically sprayed. Greece is the only country in Europe where the otter can still thrive. Elsewhere its numbers have declined as a result of man's work. In a blind drive to produce more and better, rivers are polluted by chemical fertilizers, weed killers and factory effluent, banks are cleared of trees and undergrowth. In countries which are highly developed, such as Britain, West Germany, Holland and France, the otter is rare. In Italy, it is close to extinction. If only the people who have the power to control the Greek landscape could learn from the experience of other countries that there is a point beyond which progress becomes regression and improvement deterioration. In many ways, Greece is now approaching that point, and from here true progress would be the realization that a land that is healthy for wildlife is healthy for man.

We can now make changes in our landscape which are as dramatic as Poseidon's creation of the Vale of Temple. But what we need is the goddess of wisdom.

Five male and four female lesser kestrels, Falco naumanni, *congregate on a telegraph pole, a useful resting and feeding post on the agricultural plains where they hunt. The male lesser kestrel has an unspotted back and wings but the female is easily confused with a kestrel,* Falco tinnunculus, *for she has the same spotted plumage. However, lesser kestrels are slightly smaller than kestrels and have white, not black, claws. They do not hover so frequently and tend to be gregarious and noisy, unlike the more solitary kestrels.*

Pili

Feeding on purple thistles in a grassy meadow above the village of Stournareïka are a male cardinal butterfly, Pandoriana pandora, *and a male silver-washed fritillary,* Argynnis paphia. *Behind them grows a fine candelabra thistle,* Cirsium candelabrum.

When shepherds talk of the saïta *they mean a whip snake, sometimes called a 'racer' because of its speed. It may be Dahl's whip snake illustrated here,* Coluber najadum, *the Balkan whip snake,* Coluber gemonensis, *or the large whip snake,* Coluber jugularis. *None is poisonous but all will bite a hand that comes too close.*

The town of Pili stands at the foot of the Southern Pindos mountain range. Here the river Portaïkos meets the vast plain of Thessaly before flowing into the river Pinios for its journey to the Vale of Tempe and the sea. In the sixteenth century the Blessed Vessarion, abbot of the neighbouring monastery, built a bridge: a delicate stone arch that spans the river between two tall piers. Cobbled steps lead over it, just wide enough to take a man on a mule. The river-bed lies dry and white below with occasional pools of water where small boys fish. Grey wagtails dip and dive; silver-washed fritillaries pause on pebbles. Great plane trees line the banks, then give way to firs which climb the steep sides of the gorge – dark-green splashes of colour clinging for a foothold among intricate pinnacles of rock. Buzzards hover over the jagged peaks. In this Byzantine landscape it is easy to imagine medieval travellers in flowing, coarse and richly-dark clothes riding over the bridge and through the narrow pass. The clatter of hooves on the cobbles is almost audible.

A dam has been built to hoard the water that runs down from the mountains even in high summer, and diverts it to a conduit where it flows fast towards the town. In winter the river can be a torrent, fed by the mountain snows.

The road follows the river-bed through the narrow pass and then winds into the mountains. Beyond the scattered village of Stournareïka at the head of a vast amphitheatre, work is in progress to asphalt the rough track. Swallows bathe in the dust, fluffing out their wings, pressing themselves flat to the ground, reluctant to move. At the last moment, they dart away, shining black, red and gold, like urchins fleeing from a street game. A chain of eight donkeys and mules have brought timber from the higher slopes to be piled along the roadside for lorries to take away for pulping. Here there are meadows of chicory, yellow and orange vetch, mint, purple loosestrife, white origanum, willows and poplars; higher, beech, chestnut and plane trees; and, higher still, firs. Among the firs, there are patches of open ground, pocket platforms on the mountainsides. The firs lean back against the precipitous slopes, as though digging in their toes to stop an inexorable slide into the hidden valley far below. Static in the sun, the scene is like a photograph of an intense activity. The firs, thick and black lower down, seem to be struggling upwards. Every so often, they can stop and rest by little flat green meadows, only to crowd on again upward to where a few indomitable stragglers have nearly reached the barren peaks. But the peaks are treeless; they stand aloof from the trees' puny efforts to invade their isolation. Peter is painting the most uncompromising peak of all, a hatchet-faced mountain called Tsouka. It looks as though it has been split in half by a thin-edged axe. Tracks of what could be chamois crisscross its upper reaches where thin grass clings to scree. Butterflies shimmer erratically in a meadow of bracken, purple thistles, white origanum, bright pinks. Rock nuthatches move among the firs. A buzzard flies over, with a startling crack of its wing.

A shepherd has brought two donkeys and two mules to graze on the sparse grass of a pocket platform. He has climbed up from one of the hidden villages in the isolated valley below. The fifth of seven children, he is away most of the year at school in Trikkala, but he spends three summer months at home, helping his family with their 200 sheep and goats. The animals must be guarded all the time against attack by wolves. He talks of hares, eagles, snakes – the long thin *saïta*, the 'blind' snake, and adders. He kills any snake he sees, convinced they are all poisonous. There are still bears, he says. One wandered into the centre of a nearby village a month or two ago, looking for food. Roe deer have been overhunted and now they are protected within a fence in the hills behind Pili. This is a controlled hunting area. A licence to shoot deer costs 2000 drachmas, to shoot pheasants about 500.

Lorries carry timber down from the mountains continuously. They thunder past Vessarion's delicate bridge. The small boys are now hurling sticks and stones into the river in frustration while a kingfisher sits – patient and immobile – on a rock downstream, watching fish swim in a deep, isolated pool. Nearby a big square white building advertises its function to the distant town: Countryside Taverna. The

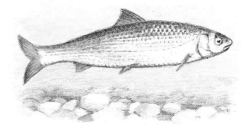

Eastern nase, Chondrostoma nasus, *which are shoaling fish of mountain streams and rivers, swim in the river Portaïkos.*

A graceful Byzantine bridge spans the Portaïkos at Pili. The river banks are overhung with the spreading branches of the oriental plane, Platinus orientalis, *a tree that is common throughout Greece and often planted for shade in village squares.*

taverna overshadows the perfectly proportioned Byzantine church of Porta Panayia. A high chainwire fence zigzags over the rocky slopes above, conserving the roe deer and pheasants.

In the evening the townspeople eat and drink and stroll up and down looking at other people eating and drinking. They talk of the thief who broke into the hotel the night before and stole video equipment bought for 8000 drachmas in Germany. As we watch the evening crowds, a mood of despair sets in, induced by the contrasts of the day: the countryside taverna overshadowing the church; the boys who had been fishing with bait and line resorting to sticks and stones and violent noise; the roe deer and pheasant fenced off so that they can be shot; the river water redirected in a conduit to leave the river-bed dry; the continuous chain of timber lorries. All are instances of the usual pattern of progress, the more efficient use of natural resources, in greater quantities, faster. Yet, like the fir trees, the butterflies and the roe deer, and like the people who strolled the town in Vessarion's day, our only function is to be born, to reproduce and to die. The difference is that we now carry out our function more efficiently, causing greater destruction. By bending nature to our own ends, we destroy it, forgetting we are part of nature too.

There is nothing beautiful in Pili but the Byzantine bridge and the Byzantine church. The people who walk its streets are less likely than their forebears to die a violent death or from illness. Their days are less physically arduous. Yet in the sixteenth century they built a beautiful bridge; in the twentieth, an ugly one. In the thirteenth century, they built a harmoniously proportioned church, filled with paintings; in the twentieth, an insensitive, ill-proportioned eating-house overshadowing it.

At the hotel a girl in her twenties wants to meet Peter. Aspasia is nervous, excited,

Black pencils of cypress mark the oval stone-walled garden of the Byzantine church at Pili, where the caretaker is scything thistles. Inside there are fine mosaics of Christ and the Virgin Mary. Frescoes blackened by a recent fire, caused by candles, are being restored. The church, Porta Panayia, dates from 1283.

desperate. All she wants to do is paint. She has no possibility at all of leaving the town to go to an art school. She works in the council offices as a clerk supporting her sick parents and her mentally-ill brother. She shows her work, and seizes avidly on remarks about perspective.

In every town there is an Aspasia; in every human, too. It does not so much make us different from the fir trees, the butterflies and the roe deer as link us to them. It is what our increasing materialism is squeezing out. It is what could save us from destructive arrogance.

All this from Pili, a most innocent backwater of a town on the fringes of the twentieth century. But because it is still on the brink of modern development, like its position at the gateway between the vast mountain hinterland and the intensively cultivated plains, it is easier to see what we are doing than in, say, Frankfurt or Sheffield.

The chamois is now rare in Greece but can sometimes be seen in wild mountain areas. It has strongly defined head markings and delicate curved horns, and its brownish-ochre coat becomes thicker and almost black in winter.

Meteora

Only the distant rim of hills that edges the vast plain of Thessaly serves as a reminder that Greece is not a single flat field growing crops in blocks. After the precipitous peaks of the Southern Pindos, with its hidden valleys and tortuous tracks, the plain glazes the eye to a state of imperception. The landscape stretches on and on, tawny, flat, ordered and empty, giving no hint of the surprise it holds in store. The sudden appearance of great, isolated pinnacles of rock emerging from the ground like misplaced stalagmites seems at first a mirage, a figment of jaded imagination. This is Meteora.

In the stormy weather of autumn and winter, the pinnacles of rock snag the lowering clouds; the monasteries built on the topmost crags may be hidden, or appear briefly above the clouds, detached from the world below in visual reminder of the way the monks used to live.

Founded during the fourteenth and fifteenth centuries, by the time of Abbot Vessarion there were as many as thirteen monasteries and about twenty smaller communities, each perched high and isolated on an individual crag, their brown-grey walls a continuation of the smooth, sheer rock face. Only welcome visitors and provisions could enter. Access depended on the monks' willingness to lower a ladder, which had to be up to 50 metres long, or let down a sling or basket by means of rope and windlass. Not until this century were steps cut in the rock faces. Now a road spills a continuous stream of visitors from cars and coaches parked so near that it would seem sacrilegious were the setting any less magnificent. But here nature and man's finest aspirations have combined to produce a landscape that can survive tourism. The chasms still exist, between the coaches and the crags, between that life and this. Here only birds can fly. In the dark air, Alpine swifts flicker, lit by the sun like dust motes. Egyptian vultures lumber heavily across the sky.

Just above the village which lies at the foot of the Meteora, linking the monastic life and the world, there is a slit in the sheer rock of the lower reaches of the nearest pinnacle. It is festooned with a line of brightly coloured red and orange cloths. It looks as though a hermit has hung up his yearly wash. A woman chopping firewood in a cottage below says no one lives there now. It is a chapel. On 23 April each year, St George's Day, boys from the village climb up a dangling rope to take down last year's cloths and hang fresh ones. Here the puzzle is, as with each pinnacle of sheer and overhanging rock: how was it climbed in the first instance to let down the first rope? At Meteora, man's ingenuity matched his spiritual aspirations.

At Meteora, where monasteries were built on isolated pinnacles of rocks during the fourteenth and fifteenth centuries, man and nature have worked together to produce a landscape of inspiring beauty.

The still waters of Lake Kerkini reflect the snow-capped Kerkini mountain range near the Bulgarian border. The lake is a wonderful place for watching birds, especially waterfowl.

North-Eastern Greece

No other part of Greece, says Tsakaridhes with enthusiastic conviction, is so rich in wildlife. He sits on his balcony overlooking the Nestos river valley, and talks of the foreign scientists who gathered here not long ago to discuss conservation.

It is a strange area. The country's second major city, Thessaloniki, sprawls at the head of the Thermaic Gulf, the natural centre of communication between Greece and her Balkan neighbours. The Halkidhiki three-pronged peninsula, an echo of the Peloponnese, attracts an increasing number of visitors. Like the part of a beach nearest a car park, it is crowded with Northern Europeans for whom the peninsula provides the first access to the Greek sea. The third and most easterly prong remains wild, however. This is Mount Athos, the Holy Mountain, the exclusive preserve of the monks and lay brethren of its twenty monasteries. Until recently, a rule made by Constantine Monomachus in 1060 was strictly observed. This forbade access to 'every woman, every female animal, every child, eunuch and smooth-faced person'. Nowadays hens, sows and female cats are allowed to live on Athos; and even beardless visitors can enter, providing they have a special permit and are male. Here, for a thousand years, God has been worshipped and nature denied. Fortunately the community had no control over wildlife's natural reproduction. Athos is probably as thickly wooded and as full of birdsong and wildlife as it was when the first monks took possession. Moreover, the monks' presence has prevented exploitation.

To the east of the Halkidhiki Greece extends for another 250 kilometres or so to the Turkish border. The land lies like a narrow pavement between long mountain ranges and the coast. This area of rolling plains of wheat and tobacco and poplar plantations might seem little more than a passageway for travellers between west and east. But it is also a passageway for wildlife. Migratory waterbirds refresh themselves on the many lakes on their way between Africa and Europe. Nowhere else in Greece provides such an abundance of habitat for waterbirds, with its salt marshes, lakes and estuaries.

Throughout history, this pavement of land has been fought over, defended and invaded. Its northern chain of mountains has formed an impenetrable line of defence, an area of strategic importance not just to man but to wildlife. The Rodhopi mountain range has been kept largely uninhabited, a buffer zone. As a result, it contains one of only three virgin forests now remaining in Europe. In these wild and remote border regions, there are bears and wolves, wild cat and lynx, rare flowers, and birds of prey; rarest of all, imperial and white-tailed eagles. It is no surprise that this area is the scene of a new invasion: that of scientists. They come to conduct field studies, mainly from foreign universities. And an international meeting to discuss conservation was arranged by a Macedonian economist and conducted on a balcony overlooking the village of Stavroupolis in the Nestos river valley.

In early spring before the trees burst into leaf the deciduous woods that cover the foothills of the Rodhopi range turn a dusky purple tinged with green. Blackthorn blossom creates the occasional splash of white. A rare white-tailed eagle soars high above the foaming green water of the river, a tributary of the Nestos.

85

The heronry of Scholari

Two plane trees, Japanese in their delicacy, are outlined against the sky near the village of Scholari. In their branches, still unmasked by leaves in April, herons are gathering for the night. This year, there are about ninety nests in one tree, twenty or so in the other.

The trees stand alone on flat land grazed by sheep. The ground is thick with yellow asphodel – and litter: rusted tins, shining tins, glass bottles, plastic bottles, tatters of polythene, blue, pink, white, green and yellow, scattered all over the dry earth, snagged on bushes, tossed by wind and carelessless far beyond the accepted town dump, the long wide ditch nearby. A man, on a wooden-wheeled cart drawn by two pale beige oxen and followed by two dark brown cows, moves slowly across the plain, down the gully and up the far side towards the village.

A car draws up on the nearby track and an excited party jumps out. They start towards the tree calling and waving to each other. The herons may well be used to noisy audiences, but it is more likely that the group will cause the departure of the very birds they have come to see. In fact, it turns out that only one member of the party is willing to approach quietly so that he can photograph the birds. He is an architect visiting his family near Scholari. His father waits in the background while the architect circles the tree, his telephoto lens trained on the nesting herons. In the tree, jackdaws and sparrows make a tremendous cacophony of sound. They share the herons' nests and their squabbling and shrieking, far noisier than that of the car party, does not disturb the true owners at all. One heron, on the topmost perch, sits with its back to the wind. With hunched shoulders and plume blown forwards over beak, it looks like the cold, bored spectator of some tedious amateur game. Another circles the tree, eyeing a possible landing place. Then it brings its legs forward and, with a slow flap of wings, comes in to land between the branches and nests and herons and sparrows and jackdaws, a large and cumbersome bird arranging itself most deftly and exactly on the chosen spot. It folds its wings as though closing a suitcase. Silhouetted against the sky stands another, with its neck arched gracefully, adding to the Japanese water-colour effect.

The man from the village says that there used to be another big tree here, but it was cut down. The herons are not protected by law, 'but we don't shoot them. They don't do us any harm.' The herons are safe as long as those two plane trees stand; protected, if not by law, then by the far more effective means of local custom.

North of the lakes of Koronia and Volvis lies the village of Scholari. Two plane trees of impressive shape and size rise from the flat agricultural plain near the village. The trees, one of which is shown here, are the home of grey herons and as many as 200 nests have been counted, though the number varies from year to year. The herons feed in the nearby lakes and fly back and forth like commuters.

The best time to watch the constant activity in the heronry is in early spring, before the leaves are out on the plane trees. Jackdaws and sparrows nest in the outer and lower twigs of the herons' nests. At dusk there is an amazing cacophony of twittering, chattering, cawing and squawking as all the birds find perches for the night.

The lakes of Koronia and Volvi

The heronry of Scholari lies between two lakes, Koronia and Volvi. Here the herons come to fish. Coots call from the pale straw-coloured reeds that stand thickly along the shores. Mediterranean gulls swoop over the blue water where numberless pairs of great crested grebes in full breeding plumage conduct their elaborate mating ritual. Very few of the grebes swim singly. Most are in pairs, facing each other. The water is like a sheet of blue paper on which the figure 2 and its reversed mirror image have been drawn a hundred times.

With an exclusive absorption, the grebes go through the formal steps of their courtship dance. With their punk-like crests erect and necks outstretched, they swim towards each other. When they meet, they dip and raise their necks several times, fluff out their feathers, shake their headdresses. Then they circle to repeat the pattern. Sometimes, in perfect harmony, they dive and reappear, holding strands of waterweed in their beaks. Treading water furiously, they manage to lift most of their bodies above the surface and, beak to beak, shake their dripping waterweed moustaches. At the moment, the waterweed is simply a symbol of intention. Later, if this particular pair do mate, they will make a nest with weed, building it up in shallow water.

Every so often, the two dive simultaneously and reappear some distance away where they seem momentarily independent of each other. But then the dance is begun again. Occasionally the pattern is disrupted by the intrusion of a single grebe who will attempt to take the place of one partner. There is an awkward triangle for a moment before one gives up, its decision hastened by a flurry of wings.

What makes the great crested grebe even more unusual is the fact that both male and female take equal part in the courtship dance. It is not only the male that sports the bright breeding colours. The female has exactly the same plumage. There is no pursuer and pursued, courtier and courted. An onlooker has no way of knowing which is the male and which the female. Perhaps the occasional disruption of the dance is caused by a similar confusion. It may be that, half-way through the ritual, two grebes suddenly realize that there is no future in this particular courtship for they are the same sex. Here is a puzzle for a party of foreign students: how does a grebe sense the sex of its dancing partner?

The long curved bill and outstretched neck of the dark glossy ibis, Plegadis falcinellus, make it instantly recognizable in flight. Below, Dalmatian pelicans stand on the shore of Lake Kerkini. The Dalmatian pelican, Pelecanus crispus, is slightly larger than the white pelican, Pelecanus onocrotalus; its plumage has a greyer tinge and its pouch is a brighter orange. In flight its black-tipped primaries distinguish it from the white pelican, which has wings edged with a broad black line.

The lakes of north-eastern Greece are the home of a large number of great crested grebes, Podiceps cristatus. Their courtship display is particularly elaborate.

Kerkini Lake

Early on Easter Monday morning, the road leads over a fertile plain empty of movement, past villages shuttered and silent, to the man-made lake of Kerkini: a still expanse of water that reflects the opaque white-clouded dome of sky and the dove-grey shapes of the surrounding hills. In the north-eastern corner of the lake, thin islands of reeds break through the water and a single tree grows from its mirror image. The crinkled skyline of the Kerkini range is highlighted by a scattering of snow. Across these bands of pale colour – of lake reflecting sky, of lake reflecting mountain, of mountain, and of sky – the pure white wings of egrets shine. Little grebes make dark shapes on the water, like printers' marks. Lines of herons, the grey and the squacco, stand elegantly on grey rocks at the water's edge. Terns shriek. A pair of pelicans, peachy-white boats in the distance, sail slowly along, long beaks tucked down on orange pouches, beak and neck of almost equal length. Sedately they turn and stretch their wings, rise lazily above the water and, their wings in slow harmonious beat, fly further away.

Gulls perch on small black fishing boats, on the oars' crossbars and on the upright gunnels. These flat-bottomed fishing boats are made of light wood covered in a kind of hessian soaked in black pitch.

Herons line the banks of Lake Kerkini. Besides grey herons, Ardea cinerea, *there are squacco herons,* Ardeola ralloides, *which appear white in flight but at rest, with wings folded, are mainly a tawny-cream. Little egrets,* Egretta garzetta, *are shown here on the lake. These are small pure white herons with black bill and legs and bright yellow feet. In the distance are little grebes,* Tachybaptus ruficollis, *and a pair of common terns,* Sterna hirundo, *fly overhead.*

The call of the cuckoo is far more familiar than the sight of the bird itself although cuckoos are common in Greece. Here one perches on the dried stem of last year's mullein.

From the thickets and poplars that line the banks, nightingales and whitethroats sing melodiously. A cuckoo pauses momentarily on the dark, upright straggle of last year's mullein, its spatulate tail dark, edged with white.

Empty cartridge cases lie on the ground below a sign which announces, upside down, that shooting is forbidden.

A pack of five dogs lollop along the lake-side track, making occasional detours to the water's edge, raising heron. The squacco heron makes a noise that is a cross between a duck's quack and a frog's croak. It is a beautiful golden tawny colour until it flies off, when its wings flash pure white. Gradually the dogs disappear into the distance of the long track, their tails wagging, very much on holiday.

A sparrowhawk flies over the lake, a small black bird in its talons, followed by a glossy ibis, a black needle of a shape, its thin, curved beak a scimitar against the sky.

The lake of Kerkini was created a number of years ago when the river Strymon which flows at the foot of the Kerkini mountains was dammed. It has become one of the finest habitats for waterbirds in Greece. The tracks and roads that circle its shores make it a particularly easy place for birdwatching, without the need for a boat. At any point along the shore it is possible to see birds in almost bewildering number and variety. Besides the herons that line the water's edge as though on guard duty, there are moorhens, coots, all kinds of duck, cormorants and various sorts of tern, mute swans, great crested and little grebes, Dalmatian and white pelicans.

This drawing shows a scene typical of Lake Kerkini. To the right is a little egret with a squacco heron beyond. On the left a marsh harrier searches for prey. Little grebes swim in mid-distance. There are various ducks: a single garganey in mid-foreground, pintails swimming in the reeds and shovelers in flight above. A black kite hovers in the distance.

Of all the waterbirds that visit or live on this man-made lake, the Dalmatian pelican is the rarest. The places where it can breed are fast disappearing. It likes to nest on reedbanks or hummocks of land in water, where it is safe from predators, in particular human ones. Fishermen do not want pelicans taking all their fish, so they protect their livelihood with guns. Others shoot pelicans for the sheer fun of it. Changes in water level have the same effect as guns on the numbers. The nesting sites disappear as wetlands are drained for agriculture, or water levels increased for irrigation. There are now thought to be less than 1000 pairs of Dalmatian pelicans left in the world. Although about 100 pairs can safely breed on Mikra Prespa in the north, a lake which now has legal protection as a nature reserve, Greece has lost seven or eight of its pelican colonies.

There is talk of increasing the level of Lake Kerkini. The reedbanks and islets of its shallow margins would disappear, and so would all the birds that live and breed among them.

The increasingly rare pygmy cormorant, Phalacrocorax pygmeus, *is the smallest European cormorant. Its head is short and lacks the white patch of the* Phalacrocorax carbo. *It favours freshwater ponds and lakes with large reedbeds.*

The delta of the Nestos

Asked in Stavroupolis where Mr Tsakaridhes might be found, the local policeman answers with some surprise, 'In his house, of course!' He cannot imagine anyone not knowing which house belongs to this most unusual of villagers.

Like Pili's Aspasia with her lonely passion for painting, and like Staras of Papingo with his collection of Vikos Gorge flowers, Tsakaridhes is a local with a special and unusual enthusiasm. His is nature conservation.

His house is reached by steep steps through a neat garden bright with narcissi, daffodils and tulips. The verandah, with views down the narrow Nestos valley, has bright red curtains bunched beside each wooden pillar. Here he sits, overflowing with information and hospitality, his address book bursting with the names of scientists. Ever since he was a boy, he has been interested in the natural world. He went to Germany as a student of economics and made his career there in finance. Now he has returned home, and has become a key link in an international chain of natural scientists who are conducting studies in the north-eastern corner of Greece. He works, in a voluntary capacity, on the economic aspects of conservation.

'There's nowhere else in Greece so good for wildlife,' he says. He is keen that studies of the area should be carried out, and not only by parties of foreign scientists. In the Rodhopi mountains, there are the three European climates in the space of 70 kilometres. New sorts of fern are being discovered. It is a depopulated area, and since the villagers have left it has become possible to see the stages of regeneration in the forest. In the remotest reaches, the trees have never been cut by man. This area of virgin forest is one of only three in Europe; there is one in Czechoslovakia, and another in Poland. The Rodhopi Forest has been a conservation area since 1978. 'But this doesn't mean anything,' he adds. Bears come down to villages on the Drama to Xanthi road to raid beehives. In the ravines of the Nestos river valley, there are sea eagles, hares and wild cats, orchids and otters. He shows a photograph of a salamander with yellow spots, and a butterfly with brilliant blue wings outspread. 'But the river is polluted – by Bulgarian factories.' There's a plan to dam the river. For a moment, his bright expression fades. There is also a plan to make a ship-breaking yard in the delta of the Nestos.

Across a plain where storks pick their way over furrows in the wake of ploughing tractors, a network of tracks leads eventually to the mouth of the Nestos. On the

Two of the woodland butterflies of central Europe and Asia that are found in north-eastern Greece are the brown and white common glider, Neptis sappho, *and the poplar admiral,* Limenitis populi.

In an unfrequented area of poplars, bramble thickets and water-filled ditches inland from the Nestos delta a Camberwell beauty, Nymphalis antiopa, *spreads its velvety wings beside a nightingale,* Luscinia mergarhynchos, *while a collared flycatcher,* Ficedula albicollis, *watches for insects beyond. The nightingale, seldom seen or heard by day in northern Europe, often sings in Greece from open perches in daytime.*

eastern bank of the broad river, a poplar plantation is ringing with birdsong of wonderful richness and variety. The bramble thickets that line a track that runs beside a reedy ditch provide just the right cover for birds. A collared flycatcher clings to the trunk of a young poplar. A nightingale perches for a moment on a bramble and turns its bright eye in enquiry, cocking its head like a robin. Its chestnut-red feathers catch the dappled sunlight among the green bramble leaves. Butterflies flicker up and down the track: speckled woods, fritillaries, small tortoiseshells, peacocks. A Camberwell beauty rocks its dramatic velvet-black wings on a pebble for a moment before dancing off into the thickets again. Frogs croak in the ditches.

The track leads out on to a marshy promontory. A fisherman's ramshackle hut stands near the water's edge. Though very few ever find their way to this eastern corner of the river mouth, the fisherman has taken the precaution of painting a warning on a rough sign: 'Do not disturb anything.' Of course he refers to his belongings. The sign could well refer to the whole area and its wildlife. From the enclosed green tunnels of the hinterland, the landscape suddenly unfolds to an immense arena of sea and sky, shining with an oyster-grey light. The wide river flows gently past ovals of little islands to merge with the sea. A line of surf marks a sandbank. Spits of pale sand interweave with reflecting water. On the western horizon, the island of Thasos rises dim and blue. A beach of fine beige sand leads the eye to the distant low eastern horizon. There is no sound, save for the splashing of

Otters need undisturbed stretches of water with thick cover where they can feed, rest and breed. Throughout Europe their numbers are declining rapidly, owing to loss of habitat and human disturbance.

A spur-winged plover, a recent colonist from Asia, stands in typically hunched position on the sands where the Nestos river meets the sea. A shelduck rests on a sandbank and common terns skim overhead.

sea on sand, the rustle of a breeze in reeds, and the calls of flocks of numberless birds. The sky is filled with the excited peep-peeps of oyster catchers, their black and white coats turning them into the most dashing of waiters. Herring gulls crowd and quarrel on sandbanks. Common terns, streamlined, split-tailed shapes, flash across the sky, uttering their sharp creaky cries. Their flight is so fast and acrobatic that they are sometimes called sea swallows. Spur-winged plovers brood thoughtfully on long legs at the water's edge. In contrast to the raucous cries of gulls and terns, the plover's cry is a demure 'chink chink'. Curlews call high above the beach. On the spits of sand and on the river's little islands, there are various ducks: the shelduck, in particular, is very smart and upright.

Once the river spread its way in numerous channels like broken veins over the whole plain. Now the delta of the Nestos is shrinking and may soon exist in name only. On the western side, the birds share their habitat with the demands of the century: a rubbish tip, a commercial fishery, a power station, efficient agriculture. Here, on the western side, the land has been drained and cultivated and a radio station built. Even so, there is still a wildness here, and the right combination of salt marsh, river and sea, thicket and wood, for vast colonies of birds to flourish.

This view of the salt marshes and lagoons near Porto Lagos gives an idea of the number and variety of birds for which this area provides such an excellent habitat and migratory resting place. From left to right: a broad-billed sandpiper, Limicola falcinellus, *on its way north; four white-winged black terns,* Chlidonias niger, *in flight; a group of spotted redshanks and common redshanks,* Tringa erythropus *and* totanus; *a Mediterranean gull,* Larus melanocephalus; *an avocet,* Recurvirostra avosetta, *one of the birds which nest here; two white pelicans,* Pelecanus onocrotalus, *the broad black line on their wings visible in flight; and a collared pratincole,* Glareola pratincola.

White storks pick their way fastidiously over the furrows left by a ploughing tractor. They feed on the worms and insects that appear in the freshly turned earth.

The crossroads of Lake Vistonis

Near Porto Lagos, where the main road runs along a narrow causeway which separates Lake Vistonis from salt marshes and the sea, the east-west movement of human traffic and the north-south movement of birds are concentrated into a visible crossroads. A stream of traffic forms the underpass, and endless waterbirds the fly-over. At times of migration, this image is accentuated, but even in mid-winter or summer, there is constant coming and going between the sea and the marshes and the lagoons and the lake. The area provides a wonderful variety of food and habitat.

Now, in April, a party of redshank and spotted redshank gather on a sandbank in a lagoon south of the road. Their plumage is changing from winter to summer colours. Soon they will leave for northern Europe. A Kentish plover, its barred buff and white feathers scarcely distinguishable from the shingly sand on which it sits as though in a nest, turns an alert eye but does not move. It is confident in its camouflage. Terns are fishing over an inlet, hovering above the water like butterflies, then plummeting into the water. Sand martins are nesting under the overhang of a sandy track above the waterline. There are Mediterranean gulls, pintail ducks, sandpipers, egrets, ruffs, and herons standing like question marks in reeds. Every so often a pelican rises heavily from a roost of 25 or so gathered on a spit of sand, and lumbers off, over the road, towards the lake. Lemon-yellow beak held out rigidly in front, wings placed far back along its body, the pelican appears as surprised as an onlooker that such a cumbersome design can fly.

This year, when the whooper swans flew in over the marshes, guns were waiting for them. Among the hummocks lie the bodies of those that fell to earth never to fly again.

A Kentish plover, Charadrius alexandrinus, *in breeding plumage is almost invisible as it nests in a shallow scrape on sandy shingle.*

Mount Falakron

The highest peaks of Mount Falakron rise to over 2000 metres and form the northern background to the plain of Drama. Falakron is a mountain with a particular and appealing quality. It holds, within not so very large an area, a spectrum of contrasting scenery. If the landscapes of Europe had to be seen in one day, then that day could be spent on and around Falakron.

An expanse of yellow asphodel covers the plain where a notice proclaims the new industrial estate of Drama. From the hem of the plain, the hills rise in rocky slopes where hellebore and cowslips flower among small bushes of juniper and rue. Large herds of goats move across the hillsides. Brushwood stockades, where goats are driven for milking and for shelter from wolves, mark out dark brown squares, like a child's drawing of a primitive camp. In a steep valley, the earth is black. Here manganese is mined. The red-roofed village of Volakas is gathered in the centre of an upland valley. Two oxen, yoked and ready for ploughing, stand patiently in a street. Above the village, terraced fields outlined with banks of small beech trees extend in amphitheatre curves of subtle colour, pale green, ochre, and misty red.

From Volakas, a new ski road leads up the mountain and into magnificent beech woods. The ground is deep in last year's copper-coloured leaves, and on the branches the new leaves are unfurling. The woods give way to rock-strewn meadows and, higher up, stony slopes faintly covered with coarse grey grass and the cheerfully shaped Macedonian pine, the tips of its even branches up-tilted as though holding candles. In a sheltered hollow by a knoll of pines, there is a group of sky-blue *Scilla bifolia* and *Corydalis solida* with its slender pink trumpet flowers.

The landscape becomes more open and windswept. There are views back down the valleys, where the foothills dip and point towards the plain of Drama. Ahead, a series of peaks, patched with snow, leads up to the ridge of one of the highest points. Its steep side is dark against a pale blue sky, its gentler slope thick with snow.

A herd of dark grey-brown, cream and beige cows moves slowly across a slope of marshy grass, their heavy bells clunking. A cuckoo calls. A pasque flower, covered in soft whitish-grey down, droops a head full of green seeds. Nearby there are others still in flower, purple bells hiding brilliant yellow stamens. A sudden splash of bluish purple on a rocky ledge just below the snow-line is a group of small pansies with yellow centres and floppy petals. Larks sing, and water pipits rise and flutter over the slopes. Black redstarts and wheatears perch on boulders. In a gully, a group of bright blue scilla and deep yellowy-orange crocus flower where the skull of a cow lies in a splodge of snow.

Melting snow has left the plateau of Ayio Pnevma a marshy expanse. In a few weeks, the ground will be thick with flowers: gentians, violas, campanulas and achilleas, many of them rare.

On the far side of the mountain, spring is well advanced. In gentle park-like terrain, masses of cowslips and hellebore flower in lush green grass beneath oak and juniper. There are birch woods, hills of mixed oak and pine and flowering white cherry. Tall sallows bend branches fluffy with yellow flowers over streams. Under hazel trees, grape hyacinths flower among shrubs of spurge and rue. The small and pretty village of Achladia lies above green meadows where the pear trees of the village's name are in brilliant white flower. As the snowy peaks of Falakron emerge out of lowering black clouds into sunshine, a double rainbow forms, creating two perfect arcs over the pastoral scene.

Two common mountain birds are the black redstart, Phoenicurus ochruros, *and the black-eared wheatear,* Oenanthe hispanica, *seen here on Mount Falakron, by a patch of flowering crocus.*

In the foothills of Mount Falakron groups of green hellebores and yellow cowslips flower in a graceful combination of shape and colour.

FLOWERS OF THE MOUNTAINS
In the many mountainous areas of Greece where grazing and cultivation are difficult, there is a wonderful variety of plants that flower from spring to autumn depending on area and altitude.

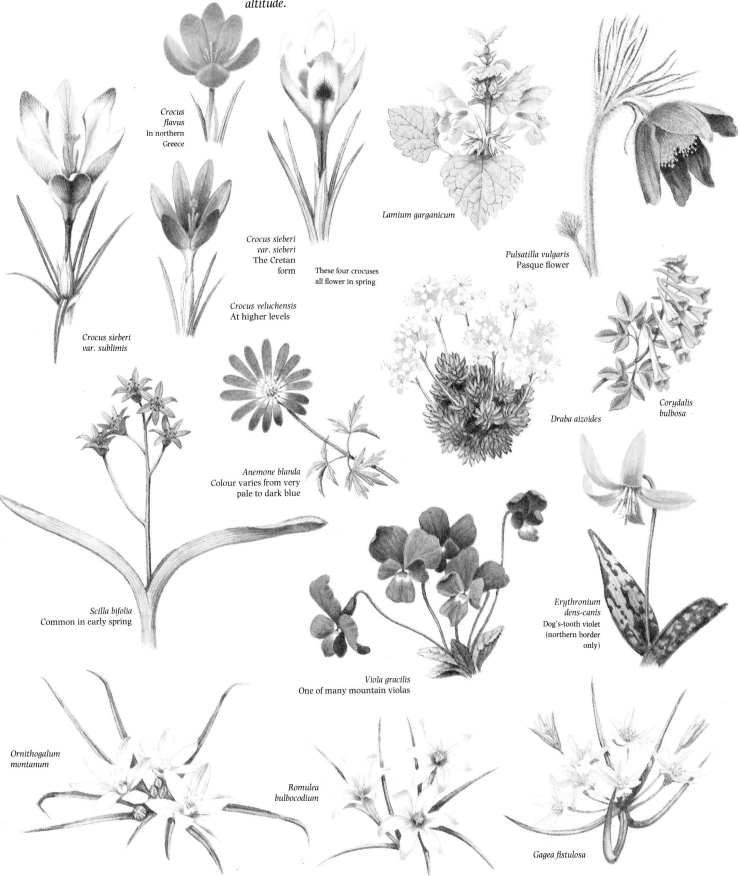

Crocus flavus
In northern Greece

Crocus sieberi var. sieberi
The Cretan form

These four crocuses all flower in spring

Crocus veluchensis
At higher levels

Crocus sieberi var. sublimis

Lamium garganicum

Pulsatilla vulgaris
Pasque flower

Draba aizoides

Corydalis bulbosa

Anemone blanda
Colour varies from very pale to dark blue

Scilla bifolia
Common in early spring

Viola gracilis
One of many mountain violas

Erythronium dens-canis
Dog's-tooth violet (northern border only)

Ornithogalum montanum

Romulea bulbocodium

Gagea fistulosa

Rodhopi

From the town of Drama, the road leads across a plain into low hills covered in thick oak and beech scrub. The wide and rushing river Nestos is crossed near the village of Paranestion, and the long climb starts into the Rodhopi mountains. A tributary of the Nestos runs green and frothing past smooth grey rocks at the bottom of a narrow valley bright with the yellow catkins of beech and the white flowers of hawthorn. An arched stone bridge crosses the green water. A sign announces

The Rodhopi forest covers a vast expanse of the Rodhopi mountain range on the Greek-Bulgarian borders. It has never been exploited by man. The thick tangle of trees, mainly beech and fir, provides an undisturbed haven for all kinds of wildlife.

thermal springs, and a smart new building stands shuttered but hopeful that people will make their way to this deserted and isolated place. Hill after hill, higher and higher, the track winds on. Oak and beech, still leafless, turn the hills purple. By three ruined houses, flowering cherries are white ghosts against the brown slopes. At each bend, the view ahead recedes in wavy lines of purple, mauve, violet and grey. There is little to relieve the eye. There is no sign of a movement. The track forks, continues, forks again. A little house appears on a crag, a row of smartly painted blue beehives on a grassy terrace below it. Then, around a corner, there is a herd of cows and an old man driving them. His blue eyes sparkle, but his smile fades when he learns that his village is not the object of the trip. 'Zagradenia? Why do you want to go up there? There's nothing to see.' The climb starts again. Hill after hill, higher and higher . . .

Now logs are stacked along the verges and tall pines march up rockier heights. There are blue shadows in deep pleats, and clumps of yellow pansies and pale purple crocus. In the shadows of pines, where snow lies in dollops of white, browning at the edges, a pinky purple flower grows in coarse damp grass. It puzzles Peter. Its single flower has six long, thin oval petals which curl back like a Dutch bonnet. From the deep yellow centre, a cluster of white stamens arch outwards, tipped with purple. The flower droops its head gracefully, the outside of its pink petals tinged yellowy-brown near the stem. Peter finally identifies it as a dog's-tooth violet, a flower he had not expected to find here or, for that matter, anywhere else in Greece.

There are pardel lynx in the more desolate reaches of the northern Greek mountains but they are seldom seen. This rare species of lynx, Lynx pardina, *is sparsely distributed in the mountains of southern Europe, mainly in Spain and the Balkans.*

A little further on, the pines and firs are interspersed with beech trees, their autumn leaves still unshed and shining copper. Slopes of dry bracken lie flattened by recently melted snow. Suddenly, this could be a beechwood in Northern Europe, and not a mountain range between Bulgaria and Greece.

Then there is a sign which marks the boundary of the virgin forest. Almost at once, the atmosphere intensifies. Perhaps the sign itself prompts awareness. But the sudden deepening of silence, and closing in of atmosphere, would be sensed with or without the sign. It is produced by the scenery itself. Although for 60 kilometres the landscape has stretched on and on without sight or sound of habitation, the few scattered ruins and the occasional areas of logging have served as reminders of human activity. Here, man has played no part in the landscape, save in making the track that continues onwards and upwards. On all sides, the forest lives and dies naturally. Firs and pines and beech straggle and struggle to the light, lean, fall, regenerate. In April, snow still bars the way into the remoter reaches. But even in the height of summer the vast tract of forest, and the wildlife that hides within its cover, remains largely inaccessible. This is nature's preserve, not man's, and long may it remain so.

In the winter months bears sometimes come down from the mountain heights to scavenge. They raid beehives for honey – and sometimes dustbins for scraps. Although they are a protected species, they are still occasionally killed.

Northern Greece

Nowhere in Greece is more than a short day's journey from the sea. In the far north, and further inland than any other place, lie two of the country's biggest lakes, Megali and Mikri Prespa. The larger of the two, as though in compensation for this inland position, emulates the sea itself. The vast expanse of water is often deep blue and choppy, the distant shores invisible, and boats are moored as though by seaside quays. The fact that two other countries border the lake, Albania to the north-west and Yugoslavia to the north-east, adds to this impression, turning the lake into an uncrossable ocean. Boats hug the southern shores. Only the waterfowl and birds in their thousands know no boundaries. They are safest, however, in Greek waters. The Prespa lakes have been designated a National Park, and their wildlife is protected. Here the Dalmatian pelican breeds.

In contrast, the harbour town of Parga on the mainland's western shores could well lie on a lake and not the sea. The narrow Corfu straits are frequently glass-calm. The island of Paxos lies just 19 kilometres offshore and with Corfu might form the boundary of a lake.

Besides a lake that looks like sea, and sea that looks like a lake, northern Greece has several other stretches of water – in particular, the lakes of Ioannina and Kastoria, in which carp, tench and eels swim and birds of many kinds live and breed.

But mainly northern Greece is a region of mountains. From the western to the eastern coast, there is range after range, remote and rugged, where wild boar, wild cats, lynx, wolves and bears can live out their days unseen and safe from man. In the deep river gorges of the northern Pindos, there are otters. Birds of prey – eagles, buzzards, vultures – sweep the skies above black ravines. In landscapes of majestic beauty, rare plants and insects flourish unwatched and scarcely recorded. It is still a place for discoveries of all kinds.

Clouds hang low over the Vikos gorge which lies west of Mount Gamila in the northern Pindos. In this landscape of spectacular beauty there are many rare plants and birds.

Opposite: a grey wagtail pauses momentarily on a boulder in the Aoos river gorge. The Vikos-Aoos National Park is a wild and beautiful region where there are otters, pardel lynx and bears, besides many impressive birds of prey such as the Bonelli's eagle, Hieraaetus fasciatus, shown in this painting.

On the way to the Zagori villages

There is a kind of rawness in Greece, a starkness. Everything appears as it is: unmitigated ugliness, unmitigated beauty. Passing through the acres and acres of Thessaloniki's industrial outskirts – wasteground and grim factories, warehouses with broken windows, tracts of bare earth, dust, grime and litter – the wretchedness of the way we have chosen to live is shown at its most depressing. There is no attempt to mask the reality, no planting of tree screens, no tidying of wasteground nor hiding of the detritus of industry. Industrial development has happened, and sprawled unchecked and unplanned wherever it can find a way.

In much the same way, the Aoos river, pent up in the ravines of the mountains, sprawls in many channels once it reaches the wide plain below Konitsa.

Heavy rain in the mountains which rise to the west of Veria sends cascades of water down every fold in the hills. The road makes its way for 250 kilometres with hardly a straightening, through the ranges of Vermio and Askio and into the northern Pindos, climbing into the clouds and down into dark valleys where the rivers tear their way westwards. Gullies in beechwoods run with sudden fast streams. Between Neapolis and Konitsa, near Pendalofos at the head of the Koutsomilia gorge, the black and brown stratified rocks catch the grey light and glisten in the rain. Waterfalls are created instantaneously. A dead oak stands black and skeletal against the dripping clouds.

Below Eptachori where the shapes and colours of the hills recall coal-mining tips, the water in the river has become the colour of dirty floorcloths. Its volume and strength is so great that it is flung back upon itself in writhing knots, forming pyramids of Medusa-like strings. In such weather, rocks fall and land slips. Nothing is safe. It is easy to understand how water shapes landscapes. The river flings itself against the piers of bridges, mounts the banks, an irrepressible force that will find its way, no matter what obstacle lies in its path. And all the time it is growing as tributaries from other mountain valleys hurl themselves into its waters.

Descending towards the plain of Konitsa, the river-bed widens and the water spreads itself in channels, carving deep cliffs in pebble islands. Suddenly ahead a startling shape appears through the cloud – a mass of rocks and snow so close that its impact is almost physical. This is Smolikas, a huge hulk of mountain, painted

Bridges such as this beautiful three-arched bridge in the Zagori area were built in Byzantine times to span the ravines and rivers of the mountains. Many still exist today along the routes of the mule-tracks that once led from village to village.

blue and grey and midnight-blue, with snow a startling white against the clouds. Its appearance is so sudden and so foreign (near the road the hills are green with dwarf beech in young leaf, fir and juniper) it seems like a giant appearing among mortals, an unexpected and outsize guest discovered to be sitting at the same table. For it rises abruptly from the plain where now the river has room to sprawl its way in many channels. On the far side of the plain the road to Ioannina climbs into the hills and once more into the clouds. Every so often the clouds lift and in the sky black and white shapes emerge, reminders that the unexpected visitor is still present, but this time in the shape of Mount Gamila.

High in these northern Pindos mountains lie the Zagori villages, their grey stone walls and roofs as much part of the landscape as the rocks among which they are built. A narrow bridge spans a river, now full to its brim and churning a greenish cream past a flat green meadow fringed with plane trees. Above, the corkscrew bends of the road gleam in the fading light like a ribbon tossed over a shoulder and, way up on the mountainside, overshadowed by the crags and sitting firmly back from the ravines that fall precipitously to the gorge below, lies a village, its stone-built houses in the twilight no more than a few pinpricks of light. Where all might be shuttered, dark and deserted, there is a log fire burning in Koulis' inn, food, wine and a welcome.

In the morning Peter sits precariously above a crevasse and sketches what he sees. This, for us, is the corner of Greece that most stirs the blood. It defies description, yet creates the urgent need to describe. It is a landscape that is like magic, constantly changing. Today, in spring, with sun and broken cloud, the shapes and colours come and go. It is at the same moment as ethereal as a vision, and as solid as the rock of which its many pinnacles and crags are made. It is the setting for Wagner's *Ring* – and a lone man, an electricity company employee, passes slowly along the hillside, collecting the leaves of chicory and dandelion for a salad.

The sound of bells fills a cobbled alleyway as cows are driven out to pasture. The houses of the Zagori villages are built of the local stone which forms blocks of unusual regularity. A particular feature of the local architecture is the roofed entrance that leads into the stone-walled courtyard of each house.

A red squirrel bounds across a path on the wooded lower slopes of Mount Gamila. In winter the ears of the red squirrel, Sciurus vulgaris, grow tufts and its reddish-brown coat becomes very dark, almost black.

The Aoos and Vikos gorges

The Aoos river, even in high summer, is a rushing powder-blue and green torrent. At the mouth of the gorge, it flows beneath a slender arched Byzantine bridge and spreads its way between banks of gravel, across the plain and northwards to Albania. Here, in the gorge, the water froths among smooth white boulders, and fish rise in pools watched by kingfishers. Grey wagtails, looking as though they stand on tightly-wound springs, bob on the rocks. Among the plane trees that edge the river, willow tits, marsh-tits and reed warblers flicker and sing. Pinnacles of rock rise on either side like organ pipes. Dark, wooded cliffs crowd above the river, receding in misty shades of smoke blue. The skyline is jagged against low cloud that swirls about the peaks.

On pale sand at the water's margin, there are the scuffed tracks of an animal. Peter looks at them closely but they are not clear enough to identify. The Aoos gorge shelters a number of animals that might have come to the water's edge last night. Besides otters, there are lynx. This is one of the very few places in Europe for the pardel lynx. It is slightly smaller and more thickly and darkly spotted than the ordinary lynx which lives in Scandinavia and Eastern Europe. The pardel lynx is confined to a few mountain areas in Spain, Northern Greece and Bulgaria. There are bears, wolves, wild cats and jackals here too. But the pad prints, spread by the night's rain, give no clue as to the night's visitor.

A man on a donkey, leading another, passes slowly along the narrow path between wooded cliffs and rushing river. He is on his way to the monastery, high up the gorge, where one monk still lives. On this August day, apart from the man on the donkey, the singing birds and the rising fish, nothing is happening here but the river.

In the Vikos gorge area at a thousand or so metres above sea level there are meadows full of flowers even in August. This painting shows such a meadow with Acanthus balcanicus, salvia, Alpine knapweed and chicory in the foreground.

A small collection of houses perched on a precipitous promontory above the Vikos gorge makes up the village of Vikos, locally known as Vitsiko. The night's thunderstorm has left the earth track between Areti and Vitsiko slippery. The track winds its way along the steep mountainside and into an open stony space. A rusty tin sign nailed to a plane tree by a fine low church grandly announces the name of this square. At first it seems that there is even less happening in Vitsiko than on the banks of the Aoos. No one is about. There is no sound from any of the houses. It is eleven in the morning.

Shining white and terracotta limestone steps lead steeply down towards the river but soon peter out in a narrow path crisscrossed with goat tracks. The path is soon lost in sliding slopes of scree. Far, far below, as though at the foot of a crumbling skyscraper, there are the faint brown shapes of goats among trees by the river. It seems impossible to move either up or down without mishap. Any moment, a foot will slip and arrival among the goats will happen far faster than intended. Stones clattering away ahead, and knees trembling, a kind of tobogganing descent continues. The goats, sitting in the shade of plane trees, some standing in the branches, watch this approach with astonishment. They, and the two young shepherds milking them, are amazed at the speed and incompetence of the descent. To them, the single path is clear, and – for the nimble-footed goats if not for the men – unnecessary.

The shepherds are making cheese, warming milk in a cauldron over a fire and straining it in punctured tins set on a frame of twigs balanced on the branch of a tree. They talk of the people who walk the length of the gorge, between Monodendri and Vitsiko. They make the place sound as busy as a city street. There are also stories of accidents, and now the gorge sounds as deserted as Antarctica. A foreigner fell high on a cliffside and broke a leg. He lay there for three days before he was rescued by helicopter.

A short distance upstream, the river-bed is dry. With the abruptness of the biblical parting of the Red Sea, the Voïdhomati rises in a series of springs and immediately covers the smooth white pebbles with sparkling blue-green water. There is no sign of the springs, just a line between the stones and a complete, flowing river.

While the Aoos gorge is impressively beautiful, it seems gloomy and forbidding, an enclosed sad and dark place, in contrast to the Vikos. Here the cliffs soar higher, but are light, airy and graceful. Even the grey wagtails that dart about the river seem livelier than those on the Aoos, their breasts flashing yellow in the sun. Bushes of Jerusalem sage, seedheads crisp cinnamon-coloured cups of ruffles like minute beehives, light the open cliffsides. There are larkspur and tiny pinks among origanum and twisted bushes of dwarf beech. Above the dry river-bed, and the springs where the boulders shine chalk-white, climb steep woods of field maple, walnut and cherry. Way above on either side run the walls of the gorge, castellated rocks, single trees dotting the high skyline here and there and clinging to sheer rock. Pinnacles are clumped like candles. There are patches of pale green among rivulets of shale; dark caves; and the rock itself is crosshatched, sometimes showing pale orange, sometimes grey, as though lit from within by the pinnacles' candles.

Top: a view of the Aoos river gorge.
Above: a stream flowing over stratified rocks forms a series of natural bathing pools.

Wild hollyhocks, Alcea pallida, *grow above a sheer drop in the Vikos gorge where crag martins,* Ptyonoprogne rupestris, *dip and dive after insects.*

About a third of the way up the gorge, another ravine cuts through the rock. When the river is flowing, the shepherds say, one can sometimes see bears and wolves at this point. They come down to drink. Now in summer the river-bed is dry and the bears and wolves are well-hidden in the wild mountain hinterland. In the shade of a walnut tree, Peter sits painting. Jays dive out of bushes, voicing their apparent horror and disgust at the intrusion. A rock nuthatch taps a confidential message on a high branch of a cherry tree. Buzzards mewl in the blue space overhead. There is an occasional call from a green woodpecker. A few cicadas creak away, singly and without the clamour of lower levels. Everywhere butterflies dance among sun-dappled boulders between the trees. A fritillary turns slowly on a pebble by a green hellebore.

The day drifts past and then, as if to corroborate the shepherds' claims, there are the sounds of an approach between the trees. But it is not the bears of the shepherds' stories, but two of the backpackers they described. They clump past in a swift and determined way. They are doing the length of the gorge.

106

The river Vikos runs in a deep gorge of spectacular beauty between the villages of Monodendri and Vikos, locally known as Vitsiko. Many rare flowers and medicinal plants grow here.

Goats, waiting to be milked, climb the branches of plane trees near the spring of the Voïdomatis river.

In the evening, outside the café which is now open, there is a lively gathering. The two shepherds are playing cards. The backpackers, young leatherworkers from Thessaloniki, relate stories of their hikes with infectious enthusiasm. They spend every holiday walking in the mountains. Their talk creates a picture of the two of them careering along the tops of mountains as though in seven-league boots, rocks clattering away from every footfall as they laugh and shout jokes at each other.

A car drives into the square, with two young couples from Serres. Tomorrow they will walk the length of the gorge. The men are keen and dressed for the occasion. The girls are vividly made-up and apprehensive. They are made more apprehensive by the tales of bears and accidents and fatal falls which the café patrons take some pleasure in relating. However, the information that the son of Ioanidhes, the café-owner, was killed by a fall is imparted in low tones. Once there flew into the square a bird the villagers call a wild cockerel and which Peter thinks might be a capercaillie. It is the bringer of bad luck. Its appearance foretells a death. The reality of tragic accidents is immediately close, until one of the lads from Serres lifts the mood with an eloquently mimed story of meeting a bear, not on a wild mountainside but on the main road to Kastoria.

Ioanidhes tells Peter of the plant-collector who lives in a nearby village. Staras has spent years collecting and pressing the flowers and plants of the Vikos gorge. A room in his house has become a kind of natural history museum. He collects butterflies as well and there is little he does not know about the wildlife of the area. He talks of 'the Vikos Doctors', the village people of the past who understood the medicinal qualities of the plants growing in and around the gorge and used them for curing illnesses. As he shows Peter specimens of Balkan acanthus, *Orchis bulgarus* and *Avamonda servica*, he compares that past interest in plants with today's. 'Now it is scientists from abroad who study the flowers. A Swedish botanist visited me once. He had been studying a single flower, an orchid, for four years! Imagine that!'

Above his village house, there are slopes green with trees: juniper and sloe, wild apple, pear and cherry, walnut, hazel, oak, Lawson cypress and dogwood. Beyond a stream, a red squirrel crosses the path – tail fluffed out, white shirtfront smart against its dark chestnut coat, ears pricked. It pauses for a moment in the branches of a hazel, its bright eyes sharp, before disappearing in the undergrowth. In a flowery and butterfly-filled meadow, Peter paints the separate hunks of engraved rock that rise into the sky from a deep ravine below the village. To the north and in the distance, there is a descending line of mountains on the far side of the gorge. Vitsiko is hidden from view, but the distinctive pile of rock on the skyline above the village is visible. From here it looks like a building, a basilica perhaps. A raven flies across the sky carrying a black shape, a replica of itself, in its claws.

There is a colossal silence. But it is a silence made up of continuous and self-absorbed sounds: the songs and calls of birds, the fluttering of wings in trees, the faint buzzing of insects and the trickling of water. The stream flows down over the terraces and eventually into a gully where it forms pools in smooth white rock. Here a curving stone wall holds a sluice gate. In summer, when the gate is closed, the pool of crystal clear water above is deep and wide enough for swimming. A tin sign on the nearby road calls this the 'Kolimbitirio', a charmingly incongruous and fabricated word for such a beautiful and natural bathing-place.

The sign is rusty; the words hard to read. Even in these days of easy travel and mass tourism, few find their way here. The ones who do are the determined and interested and, with them, the Kolimbitirio and the whole area is safe. May these words be as quiet an advertisement as the sign.

The Prespa lakes

Beyond the Aegean-blue water of Megali Prespa, which a brisk north wind whips to white peaks, the line of distant mountains belongs to Albania. The boatman points to an island, a far grey shape against the paler grey mountains. It lies in fact in the centre of this vast expanse of water. He says it once belonged to Greece, but was given to a Yugoslavian queen as a wedding present some time before the last war. He himself was acquired by Hungary in 1948. This happened to many children in those years of civil war.

Vangelis was trained in Hungary as a metal-worker. Later he worked in Czechoslovakia and, before returning to Greece, spent three years in Toronto. He relates this chequered life in a matter-of-fact fashion, betraying no sign of political preference. He is now a boatman and takes people on trips to see the birds. He seems to have as little interest in birds as in politics. When Peter asks 'What's that?' hoping to learn the Greek name for a goosander, Vangelis replies, with the satisfaction of someone imparting full and complete information, 'neropouli'. Apart from the obvious pelicans and herons, every bird is a 'waterbird'.

'The lake is 65 metres deep over there,' says Vangelis. Peter dives in to see what fish may be swimming beneath the blue surface. But it is murky and full of weed. Vangelis reports that the fishermen catch trout which often weigh six kilos: 'This big!' He spreads his hands in demonstration, but does not add 'Forgive me', as so many Greek fishermen do at what might be taken as a rude double-entendre.

He takes the boat close to the rocky shore where an icon of Ayios Nikolaos is painted on a cliff-face. A mass of Alpine swifts gathers on pink-streaked rocks nearby. A sandpiper, tiny and delicate, dances hither and thither in a crevasse by the water's edge. Goosander brood in a sandy cove. Nearby, a couple of herons perch on a rock, looking like old, tattered garments hanging from coat-hooks.

One of the small birds that breeds in the area of the Prespa lakes is the penduline tit, Remiz pendulinus. It builds its flask-shaped nest in trees on the reed-fringed margins of lakes and streams.

In every direction there is action: cormorants fly across the sky in black streaks, or dive into the water. Pelicans, both the Dalmatian and the white, rock on the surface of the water like concertina'd gondolas. Black-headed gulls shriek. There are white egrets, terns with black heads, little grebes, great crested grebes and all manner of ducks. As many as thirteen of the 28 species of bird which have been declared as threatened in Europe breed on these lakes, including the Dalmatian pelican. Even though the lakes were designated a National Park in 1974 after a 15-year-long campaign by the Hellenic Society for the Protection of Nature, neither the pelicans nor any other of the 'waterbirds' are completely safe. The people need the fish in the lake for themselves.

In the evening, cows wander back from grazing on a scrub-covered hillside, across a beach, and into the village of Psaradhes. They know their way to their byres. A woman dressed in black lets one into her yard. The cow is all she has. She weeps as she says her husband died two months ago. Her tears are not for this loss, but for her lack of money.

'I married at 15. I left my mother and married simply in order to eat. It was the occupation. We were starving. My husband fed me, but he never gave me any money. I never had any money. I have no money to pay for his last operation. Don't be like me. Get your husband to give you money.'

It is of no interest to her whether the fishermen or the pelicans catch the lake's trout; she cannot afford to buy fish. Conservation is a luxury for richer societies with a more tranquil past.

Water chestnuts grow in the still shallows of Megali Prespa. Both the Prespa lakes are rich in plants and micro-organisms.

Mikri Prespa is a valuable breeding site for spoonbills and pelicans. This view of Megali Prespa shows (from the left) a short-toed eagle, a group of ferruginous duck and tufted duck, a male and a female goosander, Dalmatian pelicans, a pair of spoonbills and a great white heron.

109

Metsovo

In the seventeenth century a Turkish vizier, escaping from the anger of his Sultan, was sheltered and helped by the people of Metsovo. Later, when the storm at court blew over, he repaid the kindness by granting the town special privileges. From 1669 to the time of Ali Pasha, the town was all but independent of the country's Turkish rulers, and able to conduct its affairs in its own way.

Now, in the 1980s, the people of Metsovo are preparing for the Festival of the Virgin Mary on 15 August. Just outside the town, a camp of nomadic Vlachs is vivid with activity. They are preparing to leave. Tents are strung with woollen blankets and rugs in glowing colours. Horses and mules stand saddled and ready. One handsome old man sits sidesaddle on his horse, his sweep of white moustache matching the long woollen socks he wears, bound with string at ankle, knee and thigh.

The town is full of families returned home for the festival. The church near the central square is the magnet, drawing everyone down steep alleyways, cobbled streets and steps to join the throng milling in and around its chanting, candlelit interior. There is a constant coming and going and exchange of greetings. It is the preparation for a party the size of a town. Those on their way to church carry prayer candles, a handful of tapers held like long-stemmed bouquets. Most of the women wear costume. Below paisley scarves, braided hair hangs in two thin plaits down the

There are still wolves roaming the mountains of northern Greece and, especially in the winter months, their howls can be heard at night. In the wilder regions, shepherds protect their flocks with guns.

The eagle owl, with its tufted ears, is easily recognized but the many species of eagles, buzzards and vultures that can be seen in the high mountains are notoriously difficult to identify. Their plumage varies according to age and season and the subtle differences in silhouette are hard to distinguish at a distance.

110

centre of the back over a blouse trimmed with braid. Sleeves are long and at the wrist extend in a deep rectangle over the hand. Black, cherry-red or bottle-green velvet V-necked bodices nip the waist above aprons which are dark and plain save for rich embroidered edges. Full skirts sway a few inches above neat stockings in dark matching colours – blue, mulberry, wine, grey or black. The skirt may be a rich brocade, a tartan, or often a zigzag pattern in black and white.

While the movement of the women is between home and church, the movement of the men is between church and square. Here they gather to sit on benches beneath the plane trees. Many wear pillbox hats in velour and navy-blue serge jackets over breeches which are wide to below the knee, then tightly buttoned to fit the leg, each tiny button covered with material. Hands and chin may rest on the carved wooden head of a mountain walking-stick which is held between wide-spread knees and clogged feet. On the upturned toes of the clogs huge black bobbles answer to the wearer's every word and movement.

As the evening progresses, the square fills. Church is over, and family parties invade. Off the square two small rows of shops form a stage set. On one side, under a colonnade, stand a cheese shop, a butcher's, a barber's and a grill-shop, each open-doored and brightly lit. The rapid comings and goings turn each shop into separate but interconnected theatrical acts. While the cook vigorously fans the charcoal, exchanging shouts with the jostling queue, cheese is weighed and wrapped, a cleaver splits a joint, and the hands of the barber flutter scissors and comb over a well-haired head. His customer, cheerful enough when he sat down, grows more and more morose as his reflection is shorn of curls.

On the opposite side of the set, a drink shop serves the tables that are crammed on stage. People crisscross between the two sides, bearing wine to drink with their grilled meat, and grilled meat to eat with their wine. Children chase each other between the tables and chairs, spin round the wooden pillars of the colonnade, fall over, are picked up, kissed, scolded. Parties arrive, meet, leave and arrive again. It is a whirligig of noise and movement, a top being spun faster and faster by sheer excitement and good humour. At any moment, the whole scene will take off – the barber, the charcoal-fanner, the tables, the wine, the beer, the glasses, the men, women and children, the rows of cheeses, the slabs of meat – all will be whipped to such a pitch that we will spin off upwards into the black night to orbit for ever, a sphere of sound and light. But each time a launch seems imminent, the momentum falters. A group gets up to leave, there is a lull before a fresh party arrives with shouts of greeting, and the ball of noise starts spinning again, faster and faster.

Metsovo lies on one side of a deep, round valley circled with rugged peaks. Perhaps its life and colour gain in intensity by virtue of its isolation, locked away as it is by range after range of encircling mountains. Yet the town is not isolated from the progress of the century. It has simply adapted to the changes in its own way. An imaginative leader stopped the drift of people to bigger towns by setting up local industries in cheese and timber. As in the seventeenth century, so in the twentieth: the people of Metsovo have a strong enough sense of their own identity and a firm enough faith in their own values to take advantage of change without being spoilt by it.

This drawing shows (top) a black vulture, with two booted eagles in different colour phases and (below) an adult honey buzzard in its barred phase. Shown with the eagle owl (opposite page) are (left) an adult lesser spotted eagle and (right) a juvenile imperial eagle.

The town of Parga

Parga's narrow winding streets are free of cars and seething with brightly coloured goods and holidaymakers. Red-roofed houses are packed tightly on the steep sides of the enclosed bay, where green islets stand reflected in blue-green water. Such a theatrical setting deserves its cast of thousands. The people and the place make a happy musical, a production that inspires good humour.

 Above the town, on a high promontory that divides a long, olive-fringed beach from the harbour, stands a ruined fortress. Swallows dip and float in the space of the sheer drop below its walls. An allium stretches out its neck over the drop, prickly purple ball of a head like a Christmas decoration hung above the dizzy height. Watching the swallows swim the air makes one's stomach turn at the temptation to imitate them. Below, a great curve of sand stretches round the translucent green sea of the bay. Behind the beach, olive groves climb the steep hillsides. The olive trees here have tall, loosely plaited trunks which are a dark brown. They look as though

Rocks and wooded islets stud the bay of Parga, a pretty harbour town on the north-western coast. The island of Paxos lies about 19 kilometres offshore.

they have been drawn with charcoal. The trunks separate the cool green shade of the leaves above from the cool green shade of the ferns below.

In the ruined fortress, it is pines that give shade to a riot of undergrowth strident with a thousand cicadas. In the entrance's covered archway, the old stones give off a cool as welcome as a long draught of iced water. The pavement stones have been polished by countless feet. They shine like sea-washed rocks.

Although it is August, the fortress is bright with flowers and greenery. Violet-blue larkspur straggle under bushes of capers. White convolvulus twines among pinky-purple mallow.

A great green lizard disappears into a bush of wormwood. Butterflies – swallowtails, walls, whites and blues – dance in dappled sunshine. A strange shrub, perhaps a milkweed, bears pale green paper lanterns, covered with soft spines. Ants crawl over the lanterns; Peter suggests they are after some sweet secretion.

Sunk into a hollow beneath the pines, the apse of a ruined Byzantine church appears in the undergrowth, the sepia patterns of paintings just visible on the crumbling stone walls. In a niche, two tins of oil are lit to the icons of St Constantine and St Eleni. Cannons lie among the rubble and the dry pine needles, some still facing the sea through embrasures in the walls, waiting for an enemy that never comes.

Nowadays, it is only boat-loads of holidaymakers from the nearby Ionian islands that cross the straits of Parga. They crowd through the streets below the fortress, like the ants on the paper lanterns. The town has an attraction for people as sweet as the milkweed has for ants.

Ants are attracted to the bristly-fruited silkweed, Gomphocarpus fruticosus, *a member of the milkweed family. This plant, now naturalized in the Mediterranean, was brought from Africa and used medicinally. Its milky juice is emetic and purgative.*

Red-rumped swallows swoop above the ruined castle of Parga, where caper flowers beside violet larkspur in August.

113

The lake of Ioannina

South of the stone-built villages of the Zagoria, the mountain of Mitsekeli hunches its shoulders above the lake of Ioannina. The lake, fed by the torrents of water that cascade down the mountain's precipitous cliffs, is about 10 kilometres long and 3 or 4 across. The large town of Ioannina is built on a promontory on the western shores. From Kalithea, appropriately called Good View, the domes and minarets of the old quarter on the far side of this smooth expanse of water, and the thick swathe of reeds along the marshy shores, create a scene more probably found in north-eastern Greece than here.

Along a raised causeway, a man is cutting reeds for basket-making. The reeds, laid out to dry, look like attenuated leeks. In a cleared channel of water, strewn with minute water-lilies, a black, flat-bottomed boat is moored. Willows and tall purple loosestrife edge a bank. Pure white convolvulus is festooned over a pale blue vetch.

Every so often there are secret ploppings in the water among the reeds, and the peepings of hidden birds. Coots suddenly make their presence known with a fight. A kingfisher bends a reed into a graceful curve with the weight of its body. It sits, upright and attentive, its head on one side. Gulls, bitterns and egrets fly around the shores of a small island where monasteries are hidden amongst trees. We ask a nun if there is still an orphanage on the island. In the winter of 1963, when the waters of the lake lay as grey and still as a steel sword, we talked about adoption while children played under the pine trees, and babies lay in rows in cots. The nun tells us the orphanage is now a kindergarten.

'Mothers work nowadays,' she says. 'They bring their children early in the morning, and collect them in the evening.'

On the skyline above the reeds, grey in the distance, is sketched the outline of two mosques, gentle domes pinpointed by tall minarets. The town has doubled in size since our last visit. An airport has been built on the plain north of the lake, where the marsh has been drained for agriculture.

'There aren't so many fish as there were,' says a taverna-keeper on the island. 'Small carp used to be able to grow big in those marshes. Now the carp spawn in the lake and the fry get eaten by other fish.'

In a tank on the taverna's terrace, there are trout from a fish-farm, carp, and a writhing knot of eels. A boat-load of French tourists arrives and makes straight for the taverna. Led by a Jacques Tati character in a funny hat, they move in their own loudly chattering circle, as enclosed in their group and as removed from their surroundings as the fish in the tank.

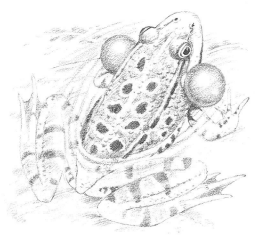

The largest European frog is the marsh or lake frog, Rana ridibunda. *Here a male is shown puffing out its greyish vocal sacs to produce its loud and varied song.*

The lake of Ioannina, despite the increasing pollution of its waters, provides a good habitat for a number of birds. In the drawing various warblers are seen among the tall stems of reeds: (top) a reed warbler, (centre) a great reed warbler, (below) a moustached warbler. On the right there is a water rail, a secretive bird more often heard than seen. Two coots swim in open water among the reeds and a little bittern flies overhead.

The butterflies of Petousi

West of Ioannina, in high mountains between Dodoni and Paramithia, there is a grove of tall plane trees filled with butterflies. Peter, who started painting butterflies when he was an 8-year-old boy, is away among the trees. On the ground lies his blue shirt, and on the peak of the upturned collar rests a little blue. It flutters off showing the periwinkle colour of its wings, and then returns to pirouette on the edge of the collar. Its closed wings are like the daintiest fan: tiny black dots circled with white on palest fawn, and trimmed with a pattern of russet on white. It has stayed most calmly and patiently for inspection – three minutes, five minutes. Then it perches on an outstretched hand, drinking from the pad of a thumb.

'An amazing little copper which I've never seen before,' says Peter, returning briefly, 'and a hairstreak.' He's off again, to watch meadow browns, small heaths, red admirals, white admirals, scarce swallowtails. The butterflies flicker over small bushes of kermes oak and hawthorn in dappled sunshine at the edge of the plane trees. A stream wanders down the centre of the grove.

The paintings show thirteen of the twenty-five species of butterflies seen in a plane tree grove near the village of Petousi. Above: southern grayling, Hipparchia aristaeus, *and woodland grayling,* Hipparchia fagi.

On bramble: pygmy skipper, Gegenes pumilio, *and nettle-tree butterfly,* Libythea celtis. *Flying: white-banded grayling,* Pseudochazara anthelea, *and eastern wood white,* Leptidea duponcheli. *On grass-stem: small heath,* Coenonympha pamphilus. *On flower: mountain small white,* Pieris ergane.

Dodoni

On thistle: Oberthur's grizzled skipper, Pyrgus armoricanus. *Flying on right: ilex hairstreak,* Normannia ilicis. *Left: Grecian copper,* Heodes ottomanus. *Right: brown argus,* Aricia agestis. *Foreground: chalk-hill blue,* Lysandra coridon.

In October the vivid golden cups of Sternbergia lutea *glisten beside the ancient theatre at Dodoni.*

The autumn afternoon sunlight slants and filters through yellowing poplars. Fields, squares of green and ochre, are outlined by dark lines of hedges and fences. The amphitheatre, grey stone patterned by light and shade, sits at the head of the valley, cocooning itself into a quiet attention towards the fields as though cupping a hand to an ear. In the valley fields, three women argue over the loading of a donkey. Their voices carry clearly to the top of the theatre. The fleece of sheep browsing beside them is haloed white by the sun. The sun turns the curving tiers of the theatre into the keyboard of an organ. The rows are not solid; the stone benches rest on blocks, so there is a pattern of dark shadows at even intervals beneath the rows. From the grassy brow of hill behind the theatre, where sternbergia flower, it looks as though a finger could depress each seat and fill the long valley with cathedral music.

The guard slumps fast asleep in his booth at the gate. It is late October and the vast coach and car parks are empty. We give a lift to a young American who had the site to himself earlier in the afternoon. He found Dodoni as wild as he hoped it would be, having come to Greece in the wake of reading such writers as Kazantzakis, Leigh Fermor and Durrell. Yet we hardly recognized the place, so tamed and organized it seemed. In our memory, it lay haphazard on a slope of barren mountainside, an immense distance from any habitation, treeless. Certainly the fencing and the car parks have appeared since our last visit – but can the landscape have changed so much? It is possible that fields have been made and some of the trees have seeded and grown in 22 years, but other trees look older. What is unchanged, and instantly recognizable, is the atmosphere. Would the shepherd who asked the oracle about the paternity of his wife's child recognize Dodoni by its atmosphere?

And might that shepherd have been a Sarakatsan? There are some who think this nomadic tribe, who speak a pure Greek, unlike other nomadic tribes of shepherds who speak Albanian-Greek, may be the original of the land. Now, in late October, when the leaves of cotinus turn crimson on the wooded hillsides, the Sarakatsani are moving down from the summer mountain pastures to the lowlands for the winter. The school in one Zagori village is closing this week; the four pupils are all Sarakatsani, and will not return until the spring. Building work will stop. The young men whose mules carry sand and cement through the narrow alleyways are leaving to spend the winter in Ioannina.

'What will you do? Will you find a job?'

Nikos shrugs his shoulders cheerfully. 'Perhaps. I did last winter.' The roads to the western plains fill with moving families and their huge herds of sheep and goats. Until a few years ago, they walked; a river of people and animals flowing west. Now the government pays a third of the cost of transport, and lorries, a bleating mass of horns and wool, form the stream. In the lowland plains, freshly built huts appear beside little houses made haphazardly of brick: the old and the new ways of home-building side by side.

Rendezvous in Kozani

There are very few towns in Greece which provide no reason at all for a visit. However featureless the buildings, however unattractive the main square, however dusty and messy the outskirts, there is usually some reason for staying: to see a nearby archaeological site; the surrounding mountains, lakes or coast; or to break a journey, start or end one. Kozani is one of the few that provide no such reason.

The clock tower in the main square strikes two o'clock on this October afternoon. Strangely there are no café tables at which to sit and wait. One glance at the only building that might conceivably provide such things is enough to banish the thought. The hotel, which outside has the dignity of a shabby and minor aristocrat, is as dark and gloomy inside as a defunct station's waiting-room. A notice above the barren desk announces, 'I am in the restaurant next door.' The restaurant next door is equally gloomy. Men sit singly at tables over plates of congealing stew. Surprisingly, the hotel is all but full. If we want to make sure of two double rooms for the weekend, we must book at once. Who on earth, besides ourselves, can be wanting to stay in Kozani?

Sharing our stone wall in the square is a pale-faced girl, waiting as we are, but for what? Having offered us a tub of rice pudding she was unable to eat, she asks, most politely, the usual questions: where are we from and where did we learn to speak as we do? Although Greek herself, she thinks of herself as a foreigner. She was brought up in Czechoslovakia. She and her family, whom she has been visiting, returned to Kozani four years ago. 'I like the Greek climate and countryside, but life in Czechoslovakia is more advanced.' She is waiting for the bus to Ioannina, where she is studying philology. Perhaps her mother or father, like Vangelis of Prespes and so many others, had been part of the *paidhomasama*, the sending of children to communist countries at the close of the civil war. The bus comes and the unanswered question lingers as we wait for our English friends. In Greece, there are constant reminders that history happens continually and is about people; the very word is Greek.

'And did your friends turn up?' asks Koulis later. Yes, they did eventually. We arrived as the clock struck two, but – 'Ha!' interrupts Koulis. 'An English hour, an English rendezvous.' The national reputation would never have produced this Greek phrase for punctuality had our friends been the sole exemplars. We have waited for Brian and Sue in many places, but none so unlikely as Kozani. The town was chosen as a possible half-way point between north-west Greece and Xanthi, where they have begun a year's teaching, their first experience of Greece beyond a holiday in the Mani. But even as a half-way point, Kozani – or rather our calculations – failed. It was a far longer journey for them, and when they did turn up, what kind of experience awaited them, what taste of Greece? We felt responsible for the litter blowing in the square, the bleakness of the surrounding landscape, the hotel's blocked lavatories and tin wardrobes, the behaviour of the other occupants, lonely boarders from Thessaloniki working at the local electricity station. As we sat talking in a bedroom, the stairwell slowly but thoroughly filled with dense dark smoke.

'It's nothing! Nothing!' came a voice from somewhere below as people gathered, reeling and choking, ready to evacuate the building. 'It's only the boiler! Nothing to worry about.' Well, this was Greek enough, even if it had the kind of Greekness that causes fond laughter in retrospect rather than the Greekness that causes wonder and admiration. That Greekness came later.

The nomadic Sarakatsan people move with their flocks of sheep and goats between summer and winter pastures, an independent way of life with strong cultural traditions. Their conical homes are made of thatch over a framework of poles, and long huts built the same way are used for storage.

On a lamppost in the square there was a faded poster advertising the museum.

'Can this be in Kozani?' asked Brian, looking at the photograph of an interesting tower-like building with overhanging wooden-buttressed top storey. 'And can that mean natural history?' he added, helped by his Ancient Greek. There was something to do in Kozani, besides talk.

But the museum was still being built. Carpenters were hammering on showcases, decorators were spraying gold paint over names engraved in marble. We were about to leave in disappointment when a man appeared. For the next two hours, Constantinos Siambanopoulos gave us a tour that could have been no more complete had the museum been finished. He led us up and down the square marble staircases, pointing out what will be where: here, a display of local costumes; there, the facsimile of a street. In the basement we were to imagine walking through a low doorway and we would be in the bowels of the earth. We would see how the rocks were formed, we would move on and up and finally off into space. The museum will be a walk through history, from the beginning of time to the present day and, in particular, the story of the people of Kozani. For the last eighteen years this local schoolmaster, now retired, has had this idea and worked towards it. He showed us storerooms full of carved wood screens, stuffed animals and birds, pottery, flints; everything he has been responsible for collecting during these years. In the banks of the river Aliakmon, he has found evidence of prehistoric man and his hunting of the animals that came to the water to drink. All the stuffed animals and birds, which include red deer, wild boar, jackal, bear, wolf, badger, wild cat, cranes and eagles, have been collected from local hunters during the last five years. He showed us round the tiny and crowded existing museum which has had to be moved several times from side street to side street but will soon have its final removal to the new building. Here, the display of local costumes is stunning. When the collection was started, a costume might have cost 2000 drachmas; now, if one can be found at all, it could cost 100,000. There are four Sarakatsani dresses which, with their black and white zigzag patterns, stand out from the rest for their beauty and craftsmanship.

The building and setting up of the museum has cost 30 million drachmas. Of this, only 5 million had to come from the government. The rest has been raised by private subscription. In the entrance hall, the names being sprayed gold are those of the 800 benefactors, local people.

When the museum opens, Kozani will provide a reason for a visit for many more people than relations, electricians and others on rendezvous. It provided us, this time, with an addition to our gallery of people with a passion. Constantinos joins Antipas of the Greek Society for the Protection of Nature, Tsakaridhis of Stavroupolis, Staras of the Zagori, Aspasia of Pili. It reminded us, too, that every corner of Greece has its surprises. At this time of year, the bare brown fields south of the town suddenly turn sky blue. It is the blue of the cultivated saffron crocus.

Jackals scavenge by night from dense cover on the edge of agricultural plains. In size and colour the jackal is midway between the larger, greyer wolf and the smaller, redder fox.

Wild boar are still common enough in well-wooded mountainous areas. Except in the breeding season, the male is solitary but females live in small groups with their distinctively striped young. They forage by night and like to rest during the day in sunny, sheltered glades.

The Ionian Islands

The stretch of the Mediterranean between the southern tip of Italy and the western shores of Greece has been called the Ionian Sea since the 6th century BC. But the islands which lie in a chain down the western Greek coast were not known as the Ionian Islands until 1800, when a Russian administrator created the title in an attempt to bring the dispersed and disparate islands into a manageable lump. Hearing the name for the first time, it is easy to imagine them lying off Ionia on the Turkish coast, or to connect them somehow with the Ionians of Attica and the Ionic style of architecture. But the name for the sea and the islands is taken from the goddess Io, and spelt with an *omikron*, not with the *omega* of Ion, the founder of Ionia.

The similarity of name, however, somehow colours the image of the islands. An Ionic column is more graceful than a Doric. An olive tree on Corfu is taller and more graceful than one on the mainland – it is very much an Ionic tree, not a Doric. Again, while Doric architecture has a masculine beauty, Ionic has a feminine one; and the landscapes of the Ionian islands, verdant and thickly wooded as they are, have a feminine charm in comparison with the masculinity of the Cyclades' stark and rugged peaks.

Here it rains more than anywhere else in Greece. Whereas in Athens the average annual rainfall is 40 centimetres, in Corfu it is 114. The high rainfall of the winter months and the more humid climate of the summer give the islands areas of greenness that last through the year. Many of the hillsides are thickly clad in a high maquis of evergreen bushes, dense thickets highlighted here and there by the tall spires of cypress. Under olive trees, drifts of wild flowers lace grassy meadows in spring, and even in summer there is a feeling of abundance about the islands. The rich vegetation feeds a host of insects, which in turn support great numbers of birds and a variety of mammals. Turtles nest on a few undeveloped Ionian beaches, and off rocky western coasts monk seals can sometimes be seen raising their round black heads from the water, like London City gents in bowler hats.

Top: a cypress wood near Fiskardho on Kefallinia.
Below: an olive grove near the Andinioti lagoon on the northern coast of Corfu.

Opposite: a swallowtail and a common blue butterfly on the wooded hillsides of Corfu.

121

Corfu

Beyond the Andinioti lagoon, where a heron flaps its wings at darting swallows and palisades trap fish, a track leads towards the northernmost point of Corfu. The land is low and moorland-like. Darkening bracken, dried bramble-thickets and purple sloes the size of grapes ramble over jagged grey boulders. A crested lark appears on the russet-earth track and skims ahead, pausing now and again to cock an eye at its followers. On it flies, a foot or two above the track, keeping to its twists and turns, then waits. As it leads the way, a sudden dampness hangs above the headland. The sun is a lamp turned low, and fingertwists of mist roll in over the grey surf. Pines are planted in strangely straight rows, wide avenues of sedge between them. Tall eucalyptus appear, dripping their leaves in the puffs of mist that float past. The land lies still, silent, other-worldly. It seems that Prospero has not lost his power to bewitch. His lark has led to grey stone walls, seven metres high. Within this broken square, pine and eucalyptus and fig have disrupted the pattern of buildings. Plumes of feather-headed sedge grow through heaps of grey stone.

A flight of steep steps leads nowhere, mullein upright in crevices. On the topmost step, a young cricket pauses. Its colours glow, a Regency dandy with suit tailored for a perfect fit: a beige oblong on its head, its front legs bright emerald with a thin black line, mid and hind legs light olive-green with a similar black line. The antennae are merest hairs, waving enquiringly around as though dismayed at the abyss beyond the step. The ovipositor looks like a poisonous talon.

Clumps of dry Jerusalem sage crowd against the arched entrance to a ruined olive-press. A fig tree twists its branches among huge timbers which once turned the massive stone, and its leaves form a canopy where once the broken beams held a roof. In one shuttered building there are neat rolls of olive nets. Before another stands a table, a grubby oilcloth tied under its lip. In the centre of this interwoven jumble of man's and nature's work stands a church. The architrave around its newly varnished wooden door is of intricately carved stone. In its curves and scrolls, bees have built nests, terracotta-coloured sandhills punctured with little round holes. Birds, flitting unseen in tall and thick bright-green pines, appear now and again among the cones which grow in clusters like pineapples from the trunk and branches. Some of the cones are newly formed and olive-green-coloured; others greyish brown, old and brittle.

In the distance the sea laps at the rocks of the headland and, under a group of graceful eucalyptus, a few fat sheep browse. Apart from the rhythmic splash of the sea, the only sounds to break the silence are the secret messages of invisible birds and insects.

Now the mist turns and blows back to sea. The setting sun appears in broken cloud making it glow like mother-of-pearl. The sea lies pale blue and wrinkled against a line of black rocks and disappears without a break into a band of white that is both sea and sky. The headland is sharply defined now: deep ochre sedge with climps of vivid green lentisc. Behind the grey stone walls of the fortified farm, a delicate line of dove-grey mountain is drawn against sky the colour of a thrush's egg. A moment later, even the roll of mist at the sea's edge lifts and dimly in the far distance rise the shapes of the Albanian mountains. Prospero has returned the ruined farm to the world.

Dark flocks of jackdaws scavenge round the shores of the lagoon. On hot, calm days, the level of water entering by the narrow channel from the sea falls and the

Marshes and stretches of open water like the Andinioti lagoon provide good habitats for the black-winged stilt. Its bright pink, extremely long legs distinguish it from its close relative, the avocet.

fish trapped in the lagoon by palisades of stout sticks and netting die of lack of oxygen. This is a loss to the men who rent the right to fish-farm in this way. Grey mullet fetch 600 drachmas a kilo, bass 900. The men, wading thigh deep, scoop the dead fish from the water and hurl them to the banks, a feast for the heron and jackdaws.

As night falls, the jackdaws leave the lagoon for their roosting place in the foothills of Pandokrator: a vast cave in a high valley hidden in the hills. The following day Stathis, from the village of Loutses, leads the way on foot. He hopes that one day someone will write about the cave and make it known to the world. In his mind's eye, he sees coachloads of tourists winding up an asphalted road and, after duly admiring the cave, refreshing themselves in his village and buying souvenirs. The cave is worth it, he promises. Mullein line the track, their yellow flowers on the tall, ungainly stalks not quite over, like half-eaten corn on the cob. Stathis points out wild asparagus. The shoots are good to eat, he says. The hillsides are rocky, a few small kermes oak and saucer-leafed Judas trees standing above the dried grasses and thistles. A few sheep huddle below in the shade of a stone pen. A single black and white kid poses momentarily on a fallen stone wall. There are very few goats on Corfu. Stathis says this is because all the people have gone away.

At a bend in the track, he turns off between rocks. Round the shoulder of the hill, the ground sinks into a circular hollow some 200 metres in diameter. Stathis points to a stony hill on the skyline. 'In the old days, lights and music were often seen up there. Nereids and *kalikantzares* playing violins...' Towards the bottom of this bowl opens a dark slit, a half-moon curve. At first it looks just large enough to warrant

The crested lark is common in dry, open country where it is more often seen running rapidly on the ground than in flight. Although even such small birds are targets for guns, it is not shy.

Barricades of bamboo and wooden poles trap the fish that enter the Andinioti lagoon from the sea nearby. Grey mullet and bass are the most common fish to swim into the shallow water of the lagoon.

the climb. The path descends steeply towards the cave. An adder curls across a rock. Further down lies a crumpled hedgehog. The ground slips more steeply below the overhang. Stathis prompts exclamations of wonder, clamouring for response to the sight. The cave itself cannot compete with his enthusiasm. He is not satisfied until a notebook and pen appear and his name and that of the cave are written down. He relaxes, confident that the coachloads of tourists are all but on their way. Attention is allowed to focus on the cave below. It is startling to see that Peter, who went on ahead, has become a blue-shirted dwarf. His figure has given the cave scale. He is the merest blue mite sucked into a cavernous black mouth. A faded red cloth hangs from a pole by the cave mouth to frighten off foxes from the goats that are penned here in winter. Hanging there limply, it looks as likely to frighten a fox as it is to ward off a violin-playing evil spirit, against which it is really intended.

The clamber down is steep and slippery, the earth soft and deep in what might be guano had it been created by sea-birds and not by goats. Stathis says the entire village took shelter here in the war from bombs. Stalactites hang from the roof. There is a slow drip of water. Ferns grow spindly in the darkness of the slimy cave floor, hart's-tongue and maidenhair. Far above, the sky at the entrance is a remote reminder, wedge-shaped, of the day outside.

'It should be lit!' cries Stathis, pointing out the shapes of the stalactites. Yet the atmosphere and thrill of a cave come from a dark mystery, a silence and a secrecy – a fragile envelope of experience easily shattered by even a single guide. If the Megali Grava were to be signposted, advertised and lit, and if access were to be made easy, would there be anything left of the cave to enjoy but its mere physical fact?

The natural beauty of the steeply wooded cliffs, inlets and coves of Paleokastritsa is unchanged. Yet the magic it held has gone, under the weight of visitors. Does the beauty of the surroundings make volleyball, windsurfing, waterski-ing, paragliding any the more enjoyable? Or does it simply provide another permutation of sun and sea? Should places of awe and beauty be kept hard to reach, so that only those who

At the hottest time of year and in the driest terrain – the edge of sandy beaches – the bulb of the sea daffodil sprouts its daffodil-like leaves and sweetly scented flowers.

Above: the Andinioti lagoon with the foothills of Pandokrator in the distance. Right: near Corfu's northernmost point fig-tree branches twist round the stones and timbers of a ruined olive press.

WARBLERS IN GREECE

A large number of the small birds that sing from the cover of olive groves, orchards, scrub and reeds are warblers. Many different species of warbler either nest in Greece or pass through during migration. The five on this page all breed here.

Fan-tailed warbler,
Cisticola juncidis
Inhabits reedbeds
and marshland

Olive-tree warbler,
Hippolais olivetorum
The region's largest warbler,
recognizable by its long beak
and pale underparts

Ruppell's warbler,
Sylvia ruepelli
The male is the only warbler of
the region with black throat as well as
black head

Orphean warbler,
Sylvia hortensis
Jet-black head and white eyes
are distinctive

Barred warbler,
Sylvia nisoria
Barred underparts and
two white wing-bars
make this warbler
easier to
identify

value the reward will struggle to reach them? This is too elitist a proposition, no doubt, for the age of jet travel and mass tourism – and how pleasant it is to travel easily and fast, and to stay in comfort. And, without Stathis as guide, the path to the cave might not have been found.

Stepping off the white, dusty road into a thick wood of olives and cypress is like dipping into a glass of cold water. High above St George's Bay, on the north-western coast of Corfu, the view of sea, distant beach, pastoral hinterland and the peaked lines of encircling hills is perfectly framed by the black spires of cypress. They stand like nails on a fakir's bed, pinning the greenery in place. Steep terraces of olives are thick in bracken, brambles and bushes of capers. Far below lies a curve of pinkish sand. The sound of the sea breaking in a single line of surf can just be heard. On the far side of the bay the land descends in a jagged line to a two-humped promontory. The sun, pale gold, is sinking towards a silver sea. Ravens give hollow croaks. Numberless birds sing in a myriad ways in the trees. A single cicada makes its presence heard occasionally. From the sea voices, tiny and distant, float upwards.

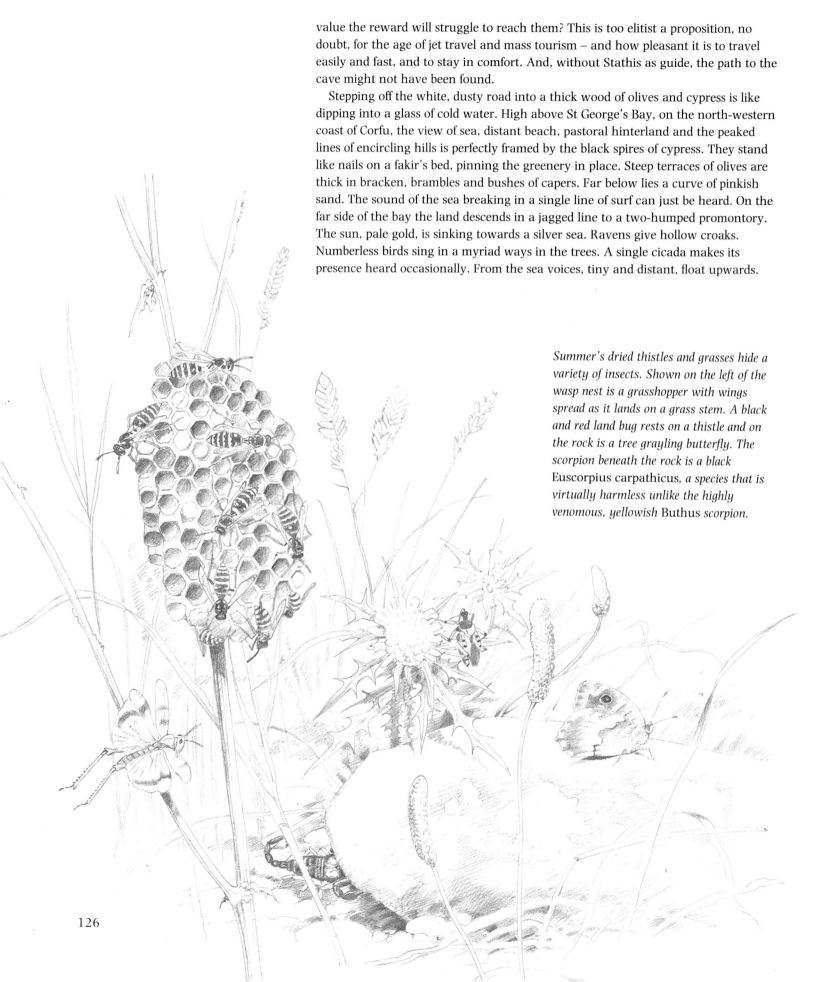

Summer's dried thistles and grasses hide a variety of insects. Shown on the left of the wasp nest is a grasshopper with wings spread as it lands on a grass stem. A black and red land bug rests on a thistle and on the rock is a tree grayling butterfly. The scorpion beneath the rock is a black Euscorpius carpathicus, *a species that is virtually harmless unlike the highly venomous, yellowish* Buthus *scorpion.*

Travelling round Corfu is like being in a maze: such a series of conical wooded hills to circle, each one thickly clad with olives and the spires of cypress. Villages are built on the sides of the hills. Their roofs of sun-faded tiles are, from a distance, like packs of falling cards. The island has so many trees that views are tantalizingly hard to come by; the sense of direction is easily lost. In the north-east corner, the island hunches one shoulder: Pandocrator is not a single mountain but rather a series of increasingly barren and viciously rock-strewn hills playing 'I'm the King of the Castle'. On the peak that wins this game, it seems almost a temporary situation. A tiny church rich in frescoes stands dwarfed under the iron feet of a television mast painted red and white. From this vantage point, the northern half of the island falls into shape, and the meanderings of journeys begin to make sense. Tourists cling to the coasts like children at a mother's apron hem. Cars and buses and bikes make their tortuous way through the hills from one coast to another.

The lagoon of Andinioti appears as a patch of silver to the north. Yesterday, not far from the lagoon on a track that leads through an olive grove, a party of ants pushed and pulled a shrivelled olive. It was not clear where they were going. There was no ant-path to be seen, nor nest. One or two ants would occasionally leave the struggling group and go ahead. Whether it was the same two who returned, it was impossible to say. Whether the main group remained the same throughout the time it took to cross the track, again there was no way of knowing. They reached the edge where a stiff line of dried grass made a barrier. It took an age to negotiate a particularly thick clump. Within the scrub there was no sign of a hole or other ants, yet they kept on zigzagging as best they could in a consistent direction. Finally – with some help, because the agony of watching their difficulties was too great – they reached a rock under which were several holes, and a feverish turmoil of ants. Had the magic been taken from the ants' arrival because their way had been made a little easier?

The suction pads on the toes of this Turkish gecko enable it to cling to smooth surfaces, even ceilings. Geckoes often live in houses, where they are useful in keeping down the insect population.

This drawing shows a dragonfly of the Libellulidae family, whose swift flight has given it the name 'darter'. On a thistle in the centre of the picture is a shield bug, and the two butterflies are a scarce swallowtail and a safflower skipper.

Lefkas

The green toad, Bufo viridis, *is often seen at night in villages. It likes to hunt for insects in the pools of light cast by street lamps or unshuttered windows.*

With the confusion of a young adult who wants to leave home as much as she wants to stay, Lefkas clings to the Akarnanian bump of the mainland with a stretch of sand and marsh at its north-eastern corner. But the sea washes over the sand, forming a large lagoon that is only a metre or so deep and turning Lefkas into an island which in its natural state would be hard to reach by either bridge or boat. A canal, thought to have been built by Corinthian colonists in the 7th century BC, had become silted up by 427 BC when the Peloponnesians, according to Thucydides, had to transport their ships over the isthmus of Lefkas. Since then every occupying power – Romans, Venetians, Turks, Russians, British and latterly the Greeks themselves – worked on the problem, dredging and building causeways. In 1905 the Greek government built the Lefkas Ship Canal, 4 kilometres long and dredged regularly to a depth of 5 metres. Now boats can pass through easily enough, and two chain ferries, plying across the narrow canal continuously, link the road from the mainland to the long causeway that leads to Lefkas town and the island.

In this area of sand spits, marsh and lagoon, pelicans and cormorants create a scene more often found on the mainland than on an island. The narrow straits, where salt pans mark the flat shores with white squares, could well be taken for an

inland lake but for the hulks of a few rusting tankers moored below the cliffs of Akarnania. But away from this north-eastern corner and the ramshackle and charming town of Lefkas, the land rises sharply. Immediately the feeling of an island prevails.

The land rises in increasingly high wooded peaks to the central height of Mount Ilias. On the highest point stands a church. Below this on a ridge, a large radar station holds its giant saucers to east and west. The circular walls of ruined windmills are just apparent among the stones of terraces and walls. At this height and on such stone-ridden land, one would not expect anything to grow. Yet the blackened skeletons of last year's mullein edge the tracks, daisies and dove's-foot crane's-bill flower, and ancient almonds blossom in wild profusion, ice-pink confections, fragile clouds of lightness that defy the harshness of the landscape. On the western side of the ridge, a flat plateau of land is neatly cultivated. Men, their donkeys tethered nearby, prune the vines that grow stunted and gnarled in the stony earth. There are patches where over the centuries stones have been painstakingly removed and wheat is now showing green.

Lower down, terraces are meadows of green studded with the white of daisies, the yellow of ragwort and, close to the ground, specks of bright blue speedwell. There is a mass of almond trees, their clouds of sugar pink blossoms a striking contrast to the solid spires of dark cypress. On this western flank, the far hills that hide the sea are barren, the colour of elephant hide, speckled here and there with a fuzz of dark bushes and spiked with cypress.

In the villages, groups of small children carry baskets of flowers from house to house, singing an Easter song, collecting money. It is a week before Easter Day.

At night, behind the bay of Nidhri, Scops owls repeatedly ask their question of the silence. The single t-woo is spaced at intervals as regular as the circling beam of a lighthouse. From reeds by the margin of a stream that runs into the sea, tree frogs break into a raucous chorus, as though in answer to the owls.

A small outcrop of rock overlooks the deep plain of olive groves beyond. Hillocks rise here and there above the misty silver green of the olives, and echo the islets that stud the bay. These little islands look like heaped tablespoons of some powdered herb in a dish of blue milk. The red-tiled roofs of Nidri just appear at the waterline, the town's length measured by cypresses. A church bell chimes faintly and a distant hammering and clunk of wood marks the position of the far boatyard.

On the western flanks of Mount Ayios Ilias the colours of blossom and wild flowers are dazzling in bright spring sunlight.

The olive-groved plain behind the bay of Nidri becomes a sea of wild flowers in spring. The sub-alpine warbler, shown singing in wild pear blossom, is more often seen among thick bushes. The butterfly spreading its wings on a rock is a southern festoon, Zerynthia polyxena.

129

In the plain the underlying hum of insects is broken every now and then by the shriek of a magpie, the hollow call of a cuckoo, or the remote crow of a cock. The ground beneath the olives glistens with the green not so much of grass as of the leaves of clover, vetch, dandelion and daisy. The tall-stalked heads of mayweed stand so thickly that they lie like swathes of white mist between the dark trunks of the olives. Bands of pale purply-pink dove's-foot crane's-bill break the white here and there, and tiny sky-blue speedwell lie in small, secret pools beneath the other weeds. *Anemone stellata* shine in the dark shadows beneath thickets of bramble and terebinth, every anemone a varying shade of pink, lilac or purple. The terebinth is just starting to flower, in russet-red clusters that look like dollops of caviar and contrast vividly with the dark green leaves. A large old cultivated pear appears wreathed in pure white blossom, a bride among the olives. The gentlest of breezes stirs its branches now and then, and a few petals drift to the daisy-white ground below.

The haunting, repetitive call of the scops owl is a familiar sound of summer evenings. This owl, Otus scops, has tufted ears and a more elongated shape than the little owl.

Star of Bethlehem and wild garlic grow in crevices of the rocky outcrop. Two huge black bees alight for a moment on a garlic flower. The bright purple flowers of a few Judas trees stand out against the greens and greys below the rock. Lemons shine in lemon trees. Jerusalem sage is coming into flower. At the base of this stony outcrop there are a few deserted farm buildings, stone walls crumbling, the brilliant purple blossom of a Judas tree bursting through a glassless stone-framed window. The pale orange and sepia tiles lie haphazard on the sagging roofs as though the merest touch would send them cascading to the stony ground. A shaggy brown donkey, its stocky legs thick with hair, stands tethered in an overgrown and roofless ruin. There is water piped to this plain; the soil is fertile and well worked in small fields among the olives and oranges. Shepherds lead small flocks of sheep and goats to graze.

Beyond Vafkeri, a village that lies along the shoulder of a wooded hill, rushing water is channelled into a reservoir and gushes unceasingly through holes into four stone washing troughs, the front stone slab of each set at a slope for pounding clothes. In the heat of summer, the green shade of an immense plane tree and the continuous and substantial flow of water make this high corner a place of refreshing respite, a startling and magical contrast to the parched earth and intense sun around. Now, in early spring, when all is green and streams flow in ravines, this corner is almost lost in the landscape. The contorted branches of the plane tree are still leafless, etched against the sky like scrawled signatures. A lesser kestrel perches on a telegraph wire, the long thin tail of a large green lizard trailing from its claw. It pecks the meat from the upper part. In the brilliant sun, it looks almost featherless save for its strongly barred black tail; the rest of the body is tawny, reminiscent of a lion. On a bank of camomile below, a festoon butterfly spreads its tigerish wings in the sun. A grassy path leads through stands of cypress and thickets of lentisc and terebinth to a tiny cemetery where clumps of white iris grow among the grasses. On the sill of a stone-carved window of the small chapel, a dandelion bursts from a crack, one head already turned to seed so early in the year. From the depths of the thickets, a warbler sings. Its song is so varied, it might be recounting lively gossip from the nearby village.

Even in the heat of summer, there are flowers on Lefkas. Floppy brown butterflies hover among yellow horn poppies on the high white western cliffs that gave the island its name: *levkos* is still a word for white. On a long, deserted stretch of beach below, colours take on an intensity as exaggerated as a falsely developed photograph. The reflection of the relentless sun on white cliffs and white sand turns the sea a brilliant opal-green and at the horizon the bluest of skies becomes a dusky rose.

The fertile plain behind the bay of Vassiliki, irrigated by pumps that send great rushing torrents of water down channels, is a verdant oasis of vegetation. White convolvulus rampages over brambles of ripening blackberries beside a dusty white track; a pebble leaves chalk-dust on fingers. Under a mulberry tree, Peter stands like Lady Macbeth, the blood-red juice of the fruit trickling down his wrist. Butterflies, various whites and small blues, dance among pale lilac scabious, the purple flowers of the chastity bush, tall cow parsley, lavender, clover flowers and yellow fleabane. A glossy chestnut horse stands tethered in a stubble-gold field, whisking its tail

Not far from the village of Vafkeri on Lefkas a stream flows down a steep gully all year long. The water, channelled into a reservoir by a large old plane tree, gushes unceasingly into four stone washing troughs, out of view in this sketch. Such places are precious in Greece even though most villages now have piped water.

A broad new road to Vassiliki now blazes its way across the hillside where Peter sat to paint this view of Mount Stavrotas.

Goats browse under magnificent palm trees in the courtyard of an old house that overlooks the plain of Vassiliki.

against flies. Nearby, curved lines of cut grass lie spiky and parchment-coloured. Beyond is a field of maize and a vineyard, recently sprayed with copper sulphate. The leaves are dusted smoky blue-green. Its far boundary is drawn by a line of variegated green: the herringbone clumps of bamboo, the feathery silver of olives, the pale mauve and grey-green cloud of the chaste tree and the black-green of cypress. Magpies and hooded crows squabble at the trees' curled fingertips. Mount Stavratos rises in the distance, serene, remote. Ravines of scree run like pleats or guy ropes holding a pale rose-grey gauze over its knobbled spine. It looks more lightly clad for the heat than our landlady Yorgoula, whose husband does not wish her to wear modern dress.

Yorgoula wears the everyday Lefkas costume in bottle-green: a dark-patterned underskirt, then a heavier plain overskirt which she lifts on either side to tie in a knot behind, like a bustle. A fringed scarf covers her from neck to bosom, and is pinned into a low braid-trimmed bodice with long sleeves. Another brownish-green scarf gracefully covers her head. She says, in answer to admiration and interest, that her dress is too hot and makes her sweat all the time. But she shows her best dresses which she made when she was 18 for her marriage. The dresses, in silk and brocade, are maroon, deep royal blue and midnight blue. The tiny pleats take one and a half days to iron. She looks after her costumes carefully, because it is no longer possible to buy such silks and brocades, nor find such good-quality gold braid.

Three palm trees grow in the walled courtyard of a fine old manor farm that overlooks the plain. It has fallen into sad disrepair. A bat hangs on the broken rafters of one room. It turns its head, twisting its bobbin of a body, flickering its ears like eyelashes. The landlord, who in days gone by owned the whole of the plain where currants grew, has died and so has his wife. The two children, grown and married, own a scent factory in Athens and do not come here. In the summer months, the

A sluggish stream behind the beach of Vassiliki supports typical summer vegetation. Convolvulus, mullein and umbellifers under the lilac spires of a chaste tree, Vitex agnus-castus, *attract a blue-winged bee, a damsel fly and a yellow-striped spider. Left of prickly* Echinops graecus *is a tree frog,* Hyla arborea.

Various species of pink grow in dry, stony places throughout Greece. This one, Dianthus arboreus, *is more commonly found in Crete and the Cyclades but was seen on a cliff in the bay of Vassiliki.*

deaf caretaker and his wife from a village in the hills above live in and around various courtyard buildings with their animals – around, because so much is outside. Saucepans, scoured bright, stand on a shelf tacked to an outside wall. A bed is made under a vine from planks covered first with terebinth leaves for padding and then with a faded cloth blanket. Another bed is a frame of logs, strewn with straw and tented over with polythene. The larder is a platform supported by poles and covered with bamboo leaves for shade. Tubs of basil and lemon balm, carnations and salvia stand against the wall. The woman in her Lefkas costume, brown headscarf, bunched apron and overskirt, gives a cockerel corn. She talks to her goats as she leads them to a fresh tethering place beneath a palm. She bends her head close to a small brown kid, her dark hands cupping its head as she tells it how good it is. The man whistles to his donkey. Panayiotis and Dhionisia have faces of contentment.

'If one has never had anything better than this, then one is happy,' they say.

Kefallinia

Lefkas and Corfu are delicate islands, graceful, fine-boned, clothed in green. In contrast, the beauty of Kefallinia is statuesque, but most awkwardly arranged. The main town and harbour lie on the coast furthest from the mainland. Huge lumps of mountains impede passage from one place to another. One whole area is divorced from the rest by invading sea, which makes it virtually another island. And the massive bulk of Mount Enos dominates the southern half, dictating long journeys which would take a raven a straightforward half-hour. Its western flanks slope in a kind of toboggan run into the sea, but flatten towards the final cliffs in tranquil terraces of fields, villages, cypresses, olives. The island has several high plateaux locked in by mountains where tilling is possible but arduous; the earth is studded with rocks and boulders. Only the Robola grape flourishes here. It thrives on thin soil, and its roots like nothing better than stones to coil around.

The soaring cliffs of the north-western coast are perhaps the most spectacular in Greece. Griffon vultures plane over the dizzy drop to the sea far below. Their size is not apparent until a warm air current sweeps them close. Then a great and ominous shadow hangs overhead. The white ruffs on their necks are visible, and the sun lights their tawny breasts and outstretched spatulate wings, fringed with black flight feathers like the fingers of burnt black gloves. It is not the time to be a stone marten, rabbit or young goat. Our passenger delights in horror stories.

'Down there,' he says, waving at a dark crevasse, 'three thousand Italians were shot by the Germans. It's called Mousehole.' He continually points out places where cars have gone over the edge and grips the dashboard as Peter, driving, turns to look. 'My cousin came off there, but he was saved by a small bush about ten metres down. A miracle. He only broke three ribs.'

He tells a Kefallinian story. In the distant past, an enemy set fire to the island at a time when enormous wild animals still lived there. The animals sought refuge on Mount Enos, where they were eventually burnt. You can still see a pile of huge bones up there, he says.

Four ravens circle over the precipitous slopes of Mount Enos. Their varying calls to each other form a conversation as confidential and satisfied-sounding as the clucking of hens over corn. What do they find to eat on this barren mountainside? The firs that clad the highest slopes stand immobile, lifeless. They look as though no wind ever stirred their waxen needles. It is hard to imagine how they can draw sustenance out of the rock-strewn ground. The bulk of the island lies below, appearing as immobile and lifeless as the firs, yet here and there small cultivated pockets of land have been terraced and the soil husbanded for centuries, cleared of as many boulders as possible. In the upland plain, where the island's Saint Gerasimos has his home, the land lies in tranquil squares of brown and ochre and green: vineyards, maize, corn stubble. On a hill beyond, ghostlike shapes show how this too was once a pattern of cultivated fields and on a further hill stands a reminder of the reason for this decay: the honeycomb walls of a once flourishing village, shattered by the earthquake of 1953. It was always hard to wrest a living from this awkward island; the devastating earthquake provided the final reason to leave, for an easier living in Australia, America or Germany. Now there is money from abroad to rebuild – not the old way of life in the inland villages, but a new way of life by the sea, a summer life of holidays.

Not far from the highest point of Enos, on a spur that commands views to the

Griffon vultures soar above the cliffs of Kefallinia

north, west and east, stands the shell of an earthquake-shattered hotel. Present-day voices exclaim at the cloud that rolls in among the firs, and call to each other from the wide terrace. They could so easily be the voices of the hotel's guests before 1953. Below the hotel the ground dips steeply, then flattens momentarily to a less harsh patch. Here, in a clearing, silver-washed fritillaries, graylings, and wall butterflies defy the inhospitable landscape and provide movement. In the spring, flowers carpet such patches, and even in August the pink tufts of *Pterocephalus parnassi* brighten the rocky ground. A coal tit pauses for a moment on the dead stump of a fir. Among the mature trees are the twisted wrecks of dead firs, and the sprightly shapes of young firs reaching for the light. This is the only surviving area of original forest in the Greek islands, and Kefallinia gave its name to this species of fir, *Abies cephalonica*. Although in atmosphere ghost-like, this is a living forest, constantly regenerating. On the terrace of the hotel, three firs have sprouted from cracks in the paving. Will man recreate the hotel for visitors to enjoy the forest, or will the forest take over the hotel . . .

A cypress wood mists a headland on one side of a deep inlet to the south of Fiskardho harbour. The trees are pencil thin and dark, stacked close. Here and there a large kermes oak billows between them and the undergrowth grows thick and unhindered by man or goats on the rock-strewn hillside. Smilax, a twining sort of ivy, arbutus with its prickly ball fruit, lentisc, terebinth and cistus form a wild woodland garden for the butterflies and birds. Graylings, wood whites and large whites flicker momentarily in sunlit patches among the lichen and moss-covered boulders. Great tits move secretly among the cypresses. At sea level the rock yawns beneath the wooded hillside, and the sea, a deeper green-blue than the hillside above, licks its way into a cave. This cave is linked by tunnels under the hillside to another with an exit further up the cliff. On the roof of the cave which overhangs the sea two fig trees have rooted in minute crevices and maidenhair fern grows gracefully among the beginnings of stalactites.

A short distance inland from the deep bay of Sami the scrubby hinterland hides a larger crater. Small olive trees teeter at the rim of the hole, their roots overhanging the sheer rock sides. Some 12 metres below gleams clear water, brilliant aquamarine in the sunlight, deepest peacock and purple in the shadows of the rock face. Sea which rushed inland at the headland of Argostoli on the western coast tunnels a way under the island and emerges here on the eastern. An entrance has been cut in

A paper nautilus is not a shell but the discarded nest of the female argonaut, a species of octopus. It is formed by a secretion which hardens to make a shelter for her eggs

135

The botanical name for the Greek fir, Abies cephalonica, *is taken from the species that grows on Mount Enos, Kefallinia.*

The adult and juvenile four-lined snakes shown here are a kind of rat snake. The wide colour and pattern variations that occur in each species at different ages and in different areas make snakes hard to identify.

the hillside nearby, and a tunnel slopes down to emerge at the bottom of the crater. Two small rowing-boats take people around the crater and then under a low rock face into a cavern. The water disappears under the rock to emerge half a kilometre away in a reedy pool behind the beach where it is channelled into the sea beneath a waterwheel. Stalactites writhe from the walls of the crater, contorted shapes in pale grey, olive-green, pink, dark sepia. Fig trees grow on a mound of fallen roof. Ferns sprout from the dripping rock face. Reflections dance on the walls of the crater. The sky is a bright distant blue circle above the rim where aerial roots drip in plumes. The water below is deep, as clear as blue glass.

Kefallinia was sometimes called Black Island because of its intense greenery. The hillsides behind Sami bear this out. Here, the maquis forms a glossy green blanket over the hills and valleys, impenetrable, ungrazed. In August, cotinus bears smoky sprays of flowers, and terebinth bunches of bright red berries. Kermes oak, which on stony heights forms low, contorted bushes which look as though they have been shaped by a crazy topiarist, grows here into small trees. There is buckthorn, myrtle, and arbutus with clumps of roughly surfaced green berries tinged with red. At Asos there is a cypress forest that has never been cut. It clothes the steep cliffs in dark green. Within the walls of the fort that surmounts the rocky peninsula, a ruined prison stands among fields and terraces, once worked by prisoners, now mostly abandoned to a riot of undergrowth. Maquis is taking over. There are bats and geckos in the cisterns which once held water for the men and the land. Perched on a dry twig is the ghost of a cicada. It looks as though it is made from spun toffee. Perfect little claws on the front legs still cling to the twig in an attitude undisturbed by the act of sloughing off its skin. It echoes the earthquake-ruined houses that cling to the island's hillsides, shells of buildings still forming villages which are roofless, tenantless.

The magnificent bastion walls of the Castle of St George were rebuilt so strongly in the early sixteenth century that no earthquake has shaken them. The castle, on a hill south of Argostoli, makes a chef's-cap shape. The walls seem to bind the top of the hill so tightly that the trees on the peak are bursting out above them, like hair above a headband. Children in the caretaker's cottage below the entrance are playing, squealing in delighted fright, with a dead snake. It is a young four-lined snake, and they say they killed it because it is poisonous, 'not like the ones at Markopoulo. The snakes of the Virgin Mary are marked with a black cross to show they are good.'

At Markopoulo, during the Festival of the Virgin Mary, there are stalls of nuts, crowds of people and a photographer. A snake is being handed round the group on the terrace below the church. Photographs are taken of people holding the snake without harm. There are expressions of delight and satisfaction: the annual miracle has occurred yet again. Every year, snakes with black crosses on their heads appear in or near the church during the week before 15 August. This year only one miraculous snake has appeared. It is a young four-lined snake, with exactly the same head markings as the one killed beneath the walls of the Castle of St George. For the villagers, the miracle is the regular and sudden appearance of the snakes and the fact that they are harmless. Yet the real miracle lies in the fact that the villagers handle them with wonder and respect, rather than hurl stones at them and crush them to death.

How powerful is the faith that renders this snake harmless in the courtyard of this church while in the courtyard below St George's Castle, and everywhere else in Greece, it is treated like his dragon.

SHRUBS OF THE HILLSIDES
Some common shrubs of the maquis are shown here bearing flowers or fruit. The flowers and fruit of the strawberry tree often appear at the same time.

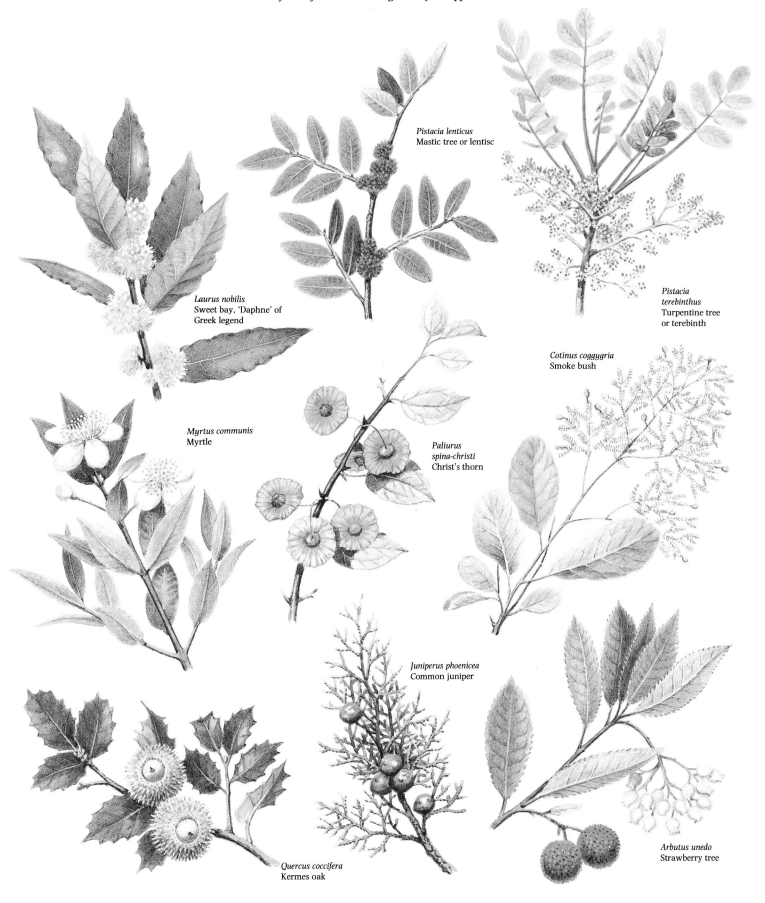

Pistacia lenticus
Mastic tree or lentisc

Pistacia terebinthus
Turpentine tree or terebinth

Laurus nobilis
Sweet bay, 'Daphne' of Greek legend

Cotinus coggygria
Smoke bush

Myrtus communis
Myrtle

Paliurus spina-christi
Christ's thorn

Juniperus phoenicea
Common juniper

Quercus coccifera
Kermes oak

Arbutus unedo
Strawberry tree

Four or five times each season, from June to August, the female sea turtle comes ashore at night to lay a clutch of about 100 eggs. After 60 days or so buried in the warm sand, the baby turtles hatch and make their way to the sea. The chances of avoiding natural predators are slim enough for the tiny turtles even without the dangers provided by humans, and this accounts for the large number of eggs laid. The two hatchlings shown entering the sea for the first time are only about 4 cm long. An adult turtle is almost a metre long and can weigh as much as 150 kg.

Most islands have at least one long sandy beach. In the past there might have been one or two fishermen's houses there. Villages seldom grew in such places. They were too vulnerable to attack by sea, and rarely provided natural harbours and safe anchorages. In the last ten or twenty years, roads have been built to such beaches and hotels and villas have sprung up, answering our demand for places to sop up the sea and sun of summer. The turtles who have always used these beaches for laying their eggs now peer anxiously out of the sea at dusk to see if the last holidaymaker has left the sand for his supper. One such long sandy beach on the southern coast of Kefallinia is still untouched by building. In the daytime a few holidaymakers may find their way there, but at night the beach still belongs to the turtles.

The setting sun drops below the foothills of Mount Enos and turns the sky a deep red. A long swell, in turquoise and pink bands, curls with rhythmic crashes on to the sand. A trail of lights appears high in the blackening humps of island, showing the position of distant Markopoulo, invisible in the daytime's sun which concentrates all attention on a close and personal circle. A sliver of moon, three days old, grows bright in the sky and with the stars throws light on sea and sand. The cool of a deep well, and the silence of a church, settles over the great expanse of night sea, sky and land. Every so often, in the scrub at the back of the beach, there are secret scurryings – perhaps stone martens – and at intervals all along the beach, some 10 metres from the water's edge, clutches of eggs, the size of pingpong balls, have been laid by turtles over the summer months and buried beneath the sand. After 63 days in the warmth of the sand, the tiny turtles hatch and with vigorous flippers and the unerring strength of instinct scrabble to the surface, over the sand and into the sea. This summer, the hatchlings emerge to find themselves in a wire cage, marked carefully and clearly in Greek and English 'Please do not disturb. Scientific experiment in progress.'

At 10 o'clock, the silence of the beach is broken by the sound of an engine. The lights of a Land Rover approach, and a group of people emerges, taking care not to break the peace either by noise or light. They make their way to a central position on the beach which has been tenanted by such a group every night since early June. They spread sleeping bags on the ground and call it Base Camp. James Sutherland, whose project this is, gives the night's instructions. They will take it in turns to walk certain lengths of the beach, watching for the arrival of mothers, and for the emergence of hatchlings. They will communicate with James and Base Camp by CB radio. There is an air of earnest enjoyment. Soon the CB crackles and an American voice reports that in nest number six there are hatchlings. James sets off along the black beach at amazing speed, followed valiantly by Tom, whose years and girth are easily double those of his leader. Tom is here for a fortnight from Vermont where he is a professor of physics. These nights on a Greek beach monitoring turtles are his holiday, volunteer work for a conservation organization. At nest number six, five tiny turtles scrabble at the base of a circular cage on the side nearest the sea. Each is

taken out in turn and, by the dim light of a red-filmed torch, its facts are taken and noted: length, carapace sections, head markings, number of claws on each flipper. While its shell is held between finger and thumb, its flippers circle vainly in the air. They feel as dry and brittle as autumn leaves. It is popped into a plastic beaker attached to a rod and scales. Weighed in at 14 grammes, and measuring 42 millimetres from tip to tail, the first baby turtle is set down on the sand like a jockey on a racecourse to flipper its way to the sea.

The work continues all night. The CBs crackle. At first light, the beach is flurried with footprints, and the minute tractor-like tracks of the turtles lead to the water's edge where now a man stands, a weighted net concertina'd under one arm. He is watching the shallows for grey mullet. Should he see a sizeable shoal, he will fling his net out and around them. Today he has not yet been lucky. He comes from Zakinthos, and views the nightly activities of the foreigners with the admirable tolerance of local Greeks to the countless thousands who come each summer to holiday among them. Turtle-watching is simply another summer-season pursuit, like volley-ball or windsurfing.

'They are marking them,' he explains, mistakenly (for they are not marked), 'to check their numbers. On Zakinthos,' he adds with an islander's pride, 'there are far more turtles than there are here.'

Behind him, a single hatchling cranes its head from a cage. It is the last to be measured and weighed before the Land Rover takes the party back to Skala for breakfast. As the sun rises, the baby turtle, left to itself, starts its journey to the sea. In the past, the sand would have been smooth. Now the footprints of the night's work present it with a terrain of deep valleys and high cliffs over which its flippers struggle valiantly, front left meeting back left, then front right touching back right. Once in the sea, the waves tumble it momentarily in froth. Then a receding wave rights it, and at once it is in its element, back flippers stretched out behind, front spiralling rhythmically. Up comes its tiny head for air, then it disappears – a scrap of life, the colour of burnt embers, the size of a coffee-cup saucer.

In the harbour master's office in Zakinthos there is a poster issued by the Ministry of the Environment: 'The protection of the sea turtle is your responsibility.' But only governments can protect the turtles – by prohibiting development on beaches such as there are on Zakinthos and Kefallinia and turning them into reserves, not only for the turtles but for the monk seals too. And would public opinion ever demand that they should?

The loggerhead sea turtle, Caretta caretta, *is under threat throughout the Mediterranean from oil pollution, trawling, exploitation, and loss of nesting habitat caused by tourism. Recent studies by Greek and foreign scientists carried out on Zakinthos and Kefallinia should make it possible for effective measures to be taken to protect the turtles' nesting grounds on sandy beaches. Nesting usually takes place during the night; the drawing below shows a mother laying eggs at dawn in the pit she has excavated with her flippers during the night.*

The Eastern Islands

The Valley of the Butterflies on Rhodes is the only place in Greece which is a well-known tourist attraction purely on the basis of its wildlife. Here in the summer months the air is thick with the bright red, black and white wings of *Euplagia quadripunctaria*, the moth that can be seen all over Greece in groves of reed mace. It is a common moth that in this one place has gained the attention of the public, simply by sheer weight of numbers and the boldness of its colours. Certainly this is a wonderful sight, but how many of the people who flock to see the Valley of the Butterflies are aware of nature in the rest of Greece, or have looked with the same admiration and attention at a single true butterfly?

Rhodes and the other islands that lie off the coast of Turkey have a particular fascination because here the flora and fauna of Asia and Europe overlap. The islands are divided for administrative purposes into two groups: the Dodecanese, which means the twelve islands, and the Eastern Sporades, the scattered islands. The Western Sporades form a distinct group of their own. They lie off the coast of the mainland near Evvia and Pilion, separated from the others by an expanse of the Aegean.

These eastern islands, lying in a north–south line so close to the shores of Asia Minor and so close to each other, might be expected to be similar in landscape and have much the same species of wildlife. But this is not the case. Each is distinctive, and there are differences not only between island and island but between one area of an island and another. Patmos, dry as it is, might well be a Cycladean island: Samos, with its woods and water, an Ionian. Rhodes, Kos, Lesbos and Chios have the variety of landscape of Greece itself, with rugged mountains, pastoral plains, pinewoods, and hillsides of aromatic bushes. This variety of habitat naturally leads to variety of wildlife. There are contrasts too in the numbers of visitors each island attracts. Some of the islands are seldom visited; others are among the most popular of the entire Mediterranean. Airports have made the long sea journey unnecessary for most, and jets fly in from Europe once, twice, even three times a day. In the long summer months, there are places where holidaymakers crowd together as thickly and as brightly coloured as the moths in the Valley of the Butterflies.

The castle of the Knights of St John, Leros.

The monastery of St John, Patmos.

Opposite: in the west of Lesvos outcrops of volcanic rock give the landscape a stark beauty. This October scene shows a rock bunting near the candelabra-shaped mullein, Verbascum sinuatum.

140

Leros

With a flash of electric blue, a kingfisher appears beneath the piers of the jetty and skims under the stern of the boat and across the paler blue water of the harbour. Beyond the low isthmus that hides the bay of Xerokambos from the port of Lakki, four misty peaks of Kalimnos appear.

Yesterday, while anchored in Xerokambos, the lively brown faces of two boys appeared at the stern of the boat: Constantine and Yannis, friends born within a few days of each other 15 years ago. They climbed on board, talking excitedly. It became clear at once that Constantine will be ready to run Greece and possibly the world – if not tomorrow, then the day after. When asked what he wanted to be, he replied, 'Lots of things. First an actor, then a lawyer. Right, I will tell you the history of Leros.' This he proceeded to do, pausing every now and again like a good teacher to check that his audience had grasped each point. 'Kalimnos and Leros were known as the good companions in the days of Homer. Homer, as maybe you know, wrote two books. Well then, in those days the island – Leros, that is – was called Lernos, which in ancient Greek meant the same as *omalos*, smooth, flat. But then it was corrupted over the years to Leros.'

The history lesson occasionally teetered as stray thoughts entered Constantine's mind. 'Have you got binoculars? You could see the Knights of St John castle from here, just by that church on the hill.' Then to Yannis, who had picked up the binoculars, he snapped, 'Hey! It's not self-service here, you know.' He took the glasses from Yannis to have a look himself. Yannis simply smiled admiringly throughout the discourse, but came into his own when the conversation turned to birds. 'Yes, Yannis knows all about birds,' said Constantine generously.

Earlier, two gulls had flown around the boat. One was a herring gull; the other had uttered a cry that was gull-like but far less shrill, a softer complaint altogether. It flew close and Peter identified it as an Audouin's gull. Its back was a pale, smooth grey, its beak red tipped with black, its legs an orangey-red. But Yannis found it hard to tally the small illustrations in the field guide with the birds he knows. He likes to go with the bird-hunters but he does not shoot the birds himself. 'Why kill birds?' he said; 'We are all part of a circle.' 'But the Greeks,' sighed Constantine, 'they won't wait for tomorrow. They do whatever they can today, whether it's good or bad.' He brought his history up to date. 'And tomorrow in Lakki there will be parades and ships in the harbour. It's the anniversary of the day when a Greek ship was bombed in the harbour.'

The port of Lakki, although still a naval base, is like a scarcely tenanted mansion. The Italians, here from 1922 to 1943, built wide roads and villas, and planted date palms and eucalyptus before the imposing buildings of their naval base, now converted into hospitals, and a high school to be inaugurated after the memorial service. The people of Leros seem to have turned their backs on this grandeur, and the life of the island is conducted on a much more intimate scale away from the main harbour. But today the islanders are flocking to Lakki for the ceremony. From dawn, there has been a continuous ferrying of sailors from a troop-carrier moored in the bay, and a mustering of the band, the brass of their instruments and the knobs on top of their white pith helmets glittering in the sun. Flags are strung from prow to stern on a patrol vessel and on the minesweeper that has slipped into place beside it. More flags flutter round a podium on the quay. A crowd begins to gather at the memorial stone. Eventually, three richly robed priests appear leading the dignitaries

The present world population of the monk seal, Monachus monachus, *is thought to be under 1000. The eastern Aegean is the main centre of population and here as elsewhere its habitat is under threat. Its ideal summer breeding ground, a totally undisturbed sandy beach, no longer exists and it now breeds in sea-level caves which are less suitable for the pups' survival.*

Audouin's gull is now very rare and the eastern Aegean is one of the few places where it may still be seen. Unlike other gulls, it prefers the open sea to coastal waters except during the breeding season, when it chooses the southern slopes of small, low islands for nesting. Its orangey-red bill divided from the yellow tip by a black bar distinguishes it from other gulls.

who will lay wreaths, the survivors of the disaster and their families, the naval guard, the boy scouts, the girl guides, and representatives from the hospitals. The bishop intones a short service, the band plays a subdued march and the National Anthem, and the names of the 80 killed are read out, in order of rank. A gun salute is fired after each section of names. A helicopter flies over, then a jet. Photographers dash here and there for good angles. The crowd, dressed in their best, laugh and chat with their friends. There is little emotional link with the ceremony for those under 50. Later some of the survivors stand before the memorial's wreaths to be photographed by their relations. One survivor who was 20 at the time, an Alexandrian Greek, still cannot sleep for more than three or four hours a night. His wife, lipstick staining her teeth, is full of the story, glorying in this annual paid holiday. 'The government used to pay for us to come here for the anniversary from Egypt. We left Egypt when Nasser came to power, and arrived in Athens with 11 drachmas to our name. My husband found work the very next day – no, he wasn't lucky. It wasn't luck that got him his job. It was his diplomas.' Does she think the day will go on being remembered? 'Oh, we'll never forget the Day of the *Olga*. As long as the survivors live. There were 75 of them, now there are about 40.' Her daughter stands beside her impassively.

From the crest of a headland on the north coast of Leros, offshore rocks and islets stand out crisply in the clear atmosphere that the north wind creates. The sea is smashed into a dark, inky blue, corrugated by the battering wind which seems to be trying to turn the blue into white. The bay of Partheni, sheltered by the headland, is a round blue pond. An occasional crack of gunfire explodes over the wavy lines of encircling hills. It is Sunday, and on Sundays and Wednesdays shooting is allowed. Five men and three dogs move slowly across the hillside. Four of the men are dressed for hunting, but the fifth, in black trousers and white shirt ballooning over his stomach, looks as though he has just woken from a snooze and wandered off. Yet he is the first to dangle a rabbit from his trouser belt. His dog has flushed it out from thick bushes of lentisc and raced after it down the hill. A sharp explosion has raised a cloud of pinkish dust which lingers on the hill as the dog races past. Then the dog drops a bundle of fur at the feet of its master. Now a second rabbit is chased from another thicket. There are two rapid shots. Crouching in the shadow of a carob tree, the man delivers a karate chop to the rabbit and hangs it on his belt beside the first. From a distance, it looks as though the man is simply the hand hired to carry the trophies of the dog's successful hunting expedition.

Not far away lies a temple to Artemis, the goddess of hunting. Searching for the ruins, the only treasure we found was the speckled starry cups of pale lilac *Colchicum variegatum*.

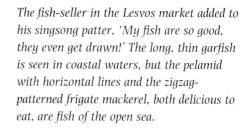

The fish-seller in the Lesvos market added to his singsong patter, 'My fish are so good, they even get drawn!' The long, thin garfish is seen in coastal waters, but the pelamid with horizontal lines and the zigzag-patterned frigate mackerel, both delicious to eat, are fish of the open sea.

From Amorgos to Kalimnos

One thousand fishing boats are registered in the harbour of Kalimnos. Fourteen of these are trawlers and 150 belong to the sponge-fishermen who are away from Easter until St Nicholas's festival in December.

Against the shafts of rising sun, the little offshore island of Nikouria is a series of sharp-edged violet and grey triangles. Eleonora's falcons still nest here but seals no longer come to the caves. Beyond the deep bay of Aiyiali the northern coast of Amorgos rises abruptly from the sea, a giant wall catching the long swell, the aftermath of days of high winds. Two hours eastwards, as the island of Kinaros appears on the horizon, the smooth surface of the sea suddenly breaks in the distance. Dolphins are arching out of the water. They have seen the boat and a moment later they are at the prow; two, then five, then seven, rolling and diving and weaving from side to side as though plaiting an invisible cord. They lead the boat through the water for five minutes. Then they disappear as suddenly as they arrived, leaving as they always do a feeling of loss, mingled with happiness and gratitude at the gift of their visit.

After the rocky hump of Kinaros has been left behind, the shape of distant Levitha is the guide. The group of buildings that houses the two families of the island can just be seen on the brow of the hill behind the deep inlet. On a journey years ago we anchored here for a night and climbed to meet the people. Then, the 4-year-old daughter of one couple stood transfixed before our own 4-year-old. She had never seen another child, and traced her fingers over Sophie's face and hair, as full of wonder as she would have been had a doll come alive.

Kalimnos from the sea looks even less capable of supporting life than Kinaros and Levitha. Its hillsides are brown and barren. There is not a hint of a bush or a tree. Yet enter the harbour, and there is an explosion of life: of noise and colour and traffic and people and boats. Fishing caiques of all shapes, sizes and colours are moored in close-packed lines, in places two or three deep, a conglomeration of nets and masts, tackle and trawling gear. On Sunday evening, the priest sings the liturgy and then preaches the sermon to the entire town by loudspeaker. His voice rebounds from the houses, which rise one behind the other in pastel shades of blues, greens, pinks and ochre. The rocky hillsides create an echo chamber for the priest; it must be as satisfactory as singing in the bath. On the quay the blaring horns of a wedding procession take over from the service. Beribboned cars push their way through the throngs of people and other traffic. More horns join the cacophony. In a corner there is a crowd around the booths of the Kalimnos Co-operative of Honey-producers. Under a banner announcing this event, a man plays the bagpipes. The bag, the stomach of a goat, is pinkish ivory in colour. The music, relayed by loudspeaker, whines and shrills above the other noises, as monotonous and insistent as the drone of the bees which produce the honey of the honey-producers.

In the still waters of early morning, the harbour is an impressionist's palette. The reflected colours tremble and shake in ripples of wind, shatter and re-form. Paint retailers must do well on Kalimnos. On each boat's basic white, the owner expresses his individuality in uninhibited use of colour. He may paint a band of brown on the sides, with a line of yellow and another of orange close to the waterline. He will turn the engine-house light blue, and pick out the windows in green; then, with a pot of scarlet, he will search for bits to highlight – a stanchion, a funnel, a lifebelt. The boats are vivid with the greens of lemons and limes, of lettuce and peppers and olives; the yellows of melons and dahlias; the blues of the sky and the sea; the reds of poppies and tomatoes; the colours of all the fruit, vegetables and flowers that are brought to the island and unloaded in shining heaps on the quay beside warehouses full of sponges and market stalls of fish.

A road leads from the harbour town of Podhia across the narrow waist of the island to Myrties and Massouri on the western coast, small seaside resorts that look across the narrow channel to Telendos. The road across the island is lined with houses and villas. In the 1950s, says the taxi-driver, there were 30,000 inhabitants. Now there are only 14,000. The wealth of the island used to come from the sponge-fishermen. Now it comes from those who have left and gone, most of them to Australia. They send back money, and visit in the summer. The impression is of a thriving, growing place despite the depopulation.

Here, where we sit above Massouri, there is the kind of background noise seldom heard in the islands. Cars pass continually up and down the distant road, and there is the roar, clatter and squeaking of building machinery somewhere down by the sea. Beneath the courtyard of a ruined cottage, overhung by a bead tree and the billowing green of a pine, a young billy-goat is tethered to a fallen branch. He bleats to a nanny and another kid tethered on the terrace below. The goats, and the cottage, belong to a time and a way of life made unnecessary for many by Australian money.

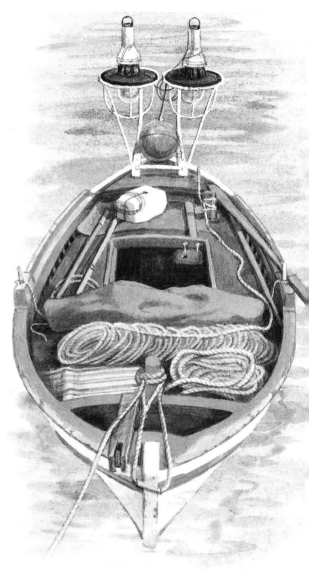

Grigri fishermen use lights from a chain of small boats to attract fish at night.

Some typical underwater life is shown in this painting. On the left: a shoal of saupe, a brown meagre (usually seen in small shoals), a moray eel emerging from its hole, and a conch shell. Grey mullet are nosing the sand in the background near a few fan mussels and a partly buried greater weaver. In the foreground there is a painted comber and, on the right, a scorpion fish and an octopus. Both the scorpion fish and the greater weaver have venomous spines. They tend to lie motionless and are hard to see. Moray eels have extremely strong teeth and can be aggressive when threatened.

145

Lipsi

There is one occupant of Paradise Cove. She sits plumb in the middle of the crescent of gritty sand. The island of Lipsi, of which the cove is part, might well be the working model for a proper Greek island. Five kilometres long by three or so wide, everything is on a small scale. One might be looking down on top of it and playing with the toy caiques in the bay, moving them about on blue plasticine waves, prodding a man on a donkey up a hill with a finger, sprinkling a hillside with a herd of goats and imitating the sound of goatbells with a fingernail on a xylophone. The working model has been made with meticulous care. The stone walls, perfectly built and maintained and topped with brushwood, enclose neat fields in which a cow or two is tethered beneath an olive, or puppies play among goats and hens. The village, the capital, is built on a hill over the harbour just as on so many proper islands. Alleyways lead round the corners and courtyards of a jumble of houses to the imposing blue-domed, bell-towered church. But it takes only a few minutes to walk up from the harbour to the church. One feels like Gulliver, but with an advantage: here visitors are luckily on the same scale as the inhabitants and the island.

This state of affairs may not last long. Since the new quay was built in 1980, buildings have sprung up. They are like those on bigger islands, large anonymous boxes, relieved by the occasional cliché of an arched verandah. They are out of scale. One is built on a headland of the bay, and dwarfs the hill on which it sits.

The name of the cove is apparent from a sign on a similar block that has risen on the low headland that separates the beach from the harbour: 'Paradise Cove Restaurant'. The signwriter had either more paint or more patience than others on the island, for he finished the job. RESTORAN VA, announces the wall of Vasillia's restaurant. Another wall was not long enough. One wonders what kind of fish FISHTAVE might be, until one sees, pushed in ignominiously below, the letters RNA.

Although the lone occupant of Paradise Cove feels anachronistic on the beach in October, she is by no means the only foreigner the working model exhibits as representative of tourism. After a man on a donkey has been trundled along the new stretch of cement road behind Paradise Cove by the model's operators, Barbara strides by in her soldier's fatigues. She first came to Lipsi in 1979 and returns whenever she can. 'She's one of us,' says Vassilia, embarrassing her with a paeon of praise. Barbara is watching the development of the island with some anxiety. Three hotels are planned. It is too small a place, she thinks, for tourism on any scale, and she has tried to convince the Greek tourist office in Switzerland and the authorities in Rhodes of this. Lipsi is far too fragile to survive many more than its present scattering of visitors. Three hotels may bring in those who holiday here this year and perhaps the Canaries next, with no thought for the background to their present enjoyment; like the Scandinavian girls who complained that there were not enough Greek boys at the discos on Rhodes. This complaint was passed on to the Greek government and announced on the news last December.

'You can't hear a word of Greek in Rhodes town any longer,' said the taxi-driver on Kalimnos. He had returned from Australia. 'Wonderful country, Australia. You can earn money and save money. The climate is excellent, the life is good, but the people . . .! Impossible. They call the English pommie bastards, and the Italians and Greeks bloody wogs. You can't live among people like that.' More and more second-generation immigrants are returning to their home islands to profit from the increased tourism. No one should want to prevent their being able to make a living

There are several species of cuttlefish and squid, soupia *and* kalamaraki *in Greek. Shown here is the sagittal squid.*

in their own country, on their families' islands. Yet in the process places as small as Lipsi can be swamped. The beauty of the landscape disappears under concrete, the islanders lose the characteristics that small communities foster, money rules and is the sole subject of conversation. How much does this cost? How much did he make? How much does he earn?

'Even in the winter nowadays,' said Costas on Sifnos, 'we don't get together and chat and sing like we did in the old days. We are all too busy with our own business, getting ready for the next season.' He spoke sadly and hopelessly. There is no going back, and he, as much as any of the others, has built and built and built. No one is at fault, and at the same time we are all at fault. Barbara, having talked of the increase in development and tourism on Lipsi, leaves to meet the weekly boat. She is expecting a group from Switzerland to whom she has recommended this as a holiday. No, they are not friends, she explains; the bank where she works also has a travel department and she made the bookings for them. In the evening, she is at Restoran Va in a white apron, helping serve her table of Swiss. And this morning the lone occupant of Paradise Cove advertises it by making notes in her notebook.

Well-maintained stone walls topped with brushwood are a feature of Lipsi and a sign that this is an island not yet totally dependent on cash from relatives abroad or tourism for survival. Local agriculture and fishing still provide much of the food for the 600 or so islanders. This drawing shows a smallholding with its threshing floor, byres, hens, goats, donkeys and cows.

Patmos

The dome of a church in the main village of Patmos is roofed with whitewashed, overlapping flat stones. The village has many fine architectural features.

The gilthead, Sparus auratus, *is a large, strong-jawed fish that feeds on crabs and shells. In the background there is a shoal of saddled bream,* Oblada melanura, *called 'black-tail'* (melanouri) *in Greek.*

Bee-eaters, swallows, crows and swallowtail butterflies float in strong air currents over the terraces that descend steeply from the white village gathered at the foot of the castellated monastery. From three ruined mills, one with a fig tree emerging from its roofless walls, the island lies below, tawny shapes interspersed with vivid splashes of blue where the sea washes into deep bays and inlets. In the harbour three steamers stand in line at the quay. They have brought tourists for the day from Samos and Kos. Barricading the sea's northern horizon, a line of islands is just visible: Ikaria, with high grey walls of cliffs, then the low humps of Fournia and, further east, a mountain leads along and down: this is on Samos.

The alleyways of the town absorb the coachloads of tourists. The maze of narrow streets, free of traffic, imposes a hush on the visitors and separates them, sending small groups singly this way and that like fish channelled through a reef of rocks. The treasures and architecture of the monastery itself have exercised this power, induced this mood of reverence.

Halfway down the hill another monastery is stacked in layers over the cave where St John had the vision which inspired the writing of the Book of Revelation. It is closed at midday until 3 o'clock. But the door opens and a grey-robed priest peers out just as two Greek women and ourselves are discussing whether we can wait. The women, who are on a day-trip from Kos, tell the priest they have come especially and have little time. The priest, with hardly a word, lets us in. He points the way through a conservatory where flowers and plants glisten from a recent watering and flagstones shine wetly. Steep steps lead down to a whitewashed terrace, where the priest pauses to ring the church bell. Then he unlocks the door of the church below. The women light candles, cross themselves three times and dip to touch the floor before each icon. A young lad, summoned by the bell, hurries in and finds the right page in the prayer book on the lectern. In response to a murmured question from the women, he joins the group under the low overhang of rock where icons hang on one wall. Set low down on the angled rockface is a narrow beaten-silver halo round an indentation. This, he explains, is where John rested his head while lying on the floor. A second silver-haloed and smaller indentation is where he rested his hands to pray. Beyond, the rockface slants inwards before the ceiling of the cave and here Prochoros wrote down the vision as John dictated, using the slanted rock as a desk. It is now covered with a tapestry. The lad points to the place in the overhang where the rock split in three with the force of the revelation. This, he tells us, symbolizes the Trinity. The women cross themselves before each relic. He shows us the icon that depicts the recumbent John and his vision. One of the women regards it with awe. She has the idea that John himself painted it. 'No, no,' says the young man, 'it was painted much later.'

The atmosphere in the cave church must surely affect every visitor, however sceptical and of whatever faith. Strong belief and reverence over centuries leave their resonance in the air.

From the summit of a craggy hill on the opposite side of the harbour valley, the layers of time are almost visible. Church bells, ringing in the monastery this Sunday, are continuing a peal begun two thousand years ago. Huge cruise ships are anchored in the bay below, while their passengers 'do' Patmos. Two waiters, in white shirts and black trousers but momentarily off duty, wandered along the quay earlier in the morning. 'Not so many Americans this year,' they said. 'President

Reagan has sabotaged our cruises.' The seven-day trip takes in Haifa in Israel as well as Rhodes and Patmos. Coaches wind through the expanding harbour village and up the ribbon of gleaming asphalt. The walls of the monastery are dark against the sun and the white cubes of houses are speckled with the black dots of doors and windows, as though the pinpoint of a pencil had pierced white nougat a thousand times. The sun throws the descending hill into a sharp relief of stone-walled terraces, dotted here and there with clumps of pine trees, indistinct and misty against the light. Down in the harbour, a crowd of people streams away from a tiny chapel which today celebrates its saint's day.

But on the summit of this hill, time belongs to the centuries before Christ. This was the hill of worship and pilgrimage, of life and death. Few come here now but goats and their shepherds, to climb the rough grey volcanic rocks that are patched with orange lichen and gleam here and there with some crystal that reflects the sun like slivers of cracked mirror. The stony ground is littered with fragments of pottery. Surely there will be a piece more special than the rest, incised or black-painted, a delicate vase lip, or the crook of a handle – something that will link us today with all those people that lived here for so long, and so long ago. Sections of their walls still stand, purple-grey blocks of stone.

On Lipsi, an old man in a straw hat was sitting on a log, watching his goats as the sun went down. He held a long black cigarette-holder in one hand. 'Listen, and I will tell you,' he began. He talked most eloquently: of corsairs, of great-grandfathers who harried the Turks during the War of Independence from hide-outs on these islands, and of the caique captain who gave thanks to the Virgin Mary on retirement at 80, saying, 'I've never made a fool of the sea, and the sea has never made a fool of me.'

'Orthodox, Catholic, Muslim, Coptic,' said Christodoulos, and pointed his cigarette-holder at the sky, 'we all worship one God. We are all people, human beings.'

A cheerful sight in many harbours is a fleet of ducks keeping a sharp look-out for offerings from the moored boats.

Patmos village, painted in October when clouds presaged the first autumn rain. The colours of the landscape of the Aegean islands vary through the year, framed by the changing blues of the sea: the summer's ochres, the winter's vivid greens.

The houses in the village of Pirgi are decorated by a method known as xysta. *Walls are plastered with a mixture that contains black sand and then whitewashed. By scraping away the top surface, the dark grey plaster is revealed. The geometric patterns often include a floral motif, perhaps a vase of flowers.*

Chios

'Look out for my son,' a woman asks us in Samos harbour as she hands a basket to a deckhand. She has sewn a cloth round the basket's brim and scrawled her son's name on it. 'He's at the Naval College on Chios. Brown hair, brown eyes, you can't miss him, he'll be waiting on the quay.'

The small tub of a steamer leaves the harbour and heads north into the wind. A handful of foreigners with backpacks prefer the fresh air of the deck. Below, a couple of women in black headscarves spread themselves and their baskets on benches, and several piratical-looking men drink coffee or arrange themselves for sleep. The *saloni* is so small and the passengers so few that food and conversation will be shared. Such journeys are social occasions, and strangers provide entertainment. A woman in a white cardigan is soon telling us how much we will like Chios; it is full of sights that on no account must we miss. The town is like Athens, with wonderful shops and tall apartment blocks. 'If you're writing a book, you'll find masses of interest on Chios.' She says she loves reading herself. 'Not like my friends who only want to talk about food and clothes. I travel a lot, and I always want to learn about the places I visit. Other people boast about the bargains they found and brought home, the leather coats and shoes and handbags in Turkey. But I read about the places, oh I'm reading all the time.' It is something of a shock to learn that she is a hairdresser, for her hair is not her best point.

'We Greeks don't read,' sighs Tassos, who has now joined the table. He is a writer, he says; a freelance journalist who specializes in tourism and economics. The

hairdresser sinks a little into her cardigan as Tassos takes over. He is an indomitable talker and time disappears in a deluge of words. Strangers do not only provide entertainment but – more important – an audience.

Greeks are wonderful talkers and teachers, and Greece is a good place for listeners and learners. But when Peter tries to correct Tassos on some wildlife misinformation, Tassos is unable to become listener and learner himself. Eventually the hairdresser spies the chance to return. Sitting herself down plump and close, she begins yet again, 'Now then, on Chios you will see . . .' But however kind and helpful her information might be, I pick up my unopened book most resolutely and whisper that Peter needs sleep.

On Chios you will see (the words cling, a chant in the mind) medieval fortress towns, mastic villages, and *xysta*. Wandering around the village of Pirgi is like being let loose in a cage of zebras. Every possible surface of every possible building has been decorated with black and white geometric designs. The houses look as though they have adopted a camouflage of light and shade to hide against the stark rocky landscape. Tiny red tomatoes hang in strings from balconies, drying for the winter months. Women crouch in dark doorways, knees spread beneath aprons, sorting mastic from leaf debris on large flat sieves. Pirgi is one of the mastic villages of Chios. Only in this south-western region of the island does the lentisc give such good resin. The bushes, which elsewhere in Greece sprawl thickly on the ground, are planted on the hillside terraces like olives or vines and pruned so that they become small trees. With bare trunks and branches twisting beneath a canopy of green, they look like bonsai trees, giant evergreens miniaturized by Japanese gardeners.

Not far from the village, a donkey is tethered by a stone wall and a man lies beneath a lentisc on the terrace beyond, chipping the resin from the bark with a spatula. He sweeps up the fallen pieces with a bunch of twigs. The globules of resin look like diamonds melted by the sun. Work on the lentisc terraces starts, he says, on 1 June. First, they clean up the winter's debris of fallen leaves to leave the red earth clear beneath each tree. Then they make incisions in the bark and spend two or three months scraping and collecting the resin. It is the women's work, during the winter months, to clean and sort the mastic. Ants swarm around the trees and sometimes get caught and crystallized. He gives us a generous handful of the gum to chew; the rate at the moment is 2500 drachmas a kilo, and collecting and cleaning is a slow, laborious business.

The villages smell of mastic, a fresh, pungent, addictive scent. They are medieval fortress villages, built within stout walls and far enough from the sea to have been safe from pirates. In Mesta, which lies squat and brown among squat, brown hills, narrow alleyways lead beneath arches to a group making *raki* in a courtyard. They are set up for the day with a table, coffee, grapes, and glasses to test the spirit. Over a crackling fire of hefty logs hangs a closed cauldron in which a mush of figs and old wine is boiling. A copper pipe leads the steam through a tank of cold water to a tap at the base. The group round the fire is growing happier as the day progresses, calling to passers-by to try a glass. The liquid could launch a spaceship. The mere fumes are enough to intoxicate. Message to hairdresser: after *raki* in Mesta, on Chios you will see little else.

Mesta, a medieval fortress town, is in the mastic-producing area of Chios. In an alleyway a woman is sorting and cleaning the mastic on a sieve.

Resin is collected from lentisc bushes. Called mastic, it is used to make a sticky sweet and chewing-gum, and to flavour liqueur.

Samos

Samos is an island of woods and water. In winter there are rushing rivers and even in the dry months streams flow in shady gullies. The sketch is of such a stream in the foothills of Kerkis near Nikoloudhes.

The steep valley behind the village of Kokkari is full of trees – walnuts, cherries, chestnuts, cypresses, olives, poplars and planes.

Where a shaft of sunlight penetrates the foliage and falls on the stiller shallows of the stream, there are strange black blobs rimmed with light. They lie in groups of six, two large and four small, and every so often flick out and away to reform. They look like the miniature footprints of a panda. In fact they are the shadows cast by water-boatmen on the surface some distance away from their reflections.

The stream tumbles down a ravine between thickly wooded hills, forming waterfalls between boulders as it drops. The banks are crowded with maidenhair fern, bracken, ivy and cyclamen in leaf litter. There are oleander, cypresses, buckthorn and a tangle of undergrowth festooned with cobwebs shining silver where the sun penetrates. On the far side of the stream, an ancient stone wall clings to the bank, defying gravity and time. Dripping over it like a tattered curtain, tree roots and earth, moss and ivy hang in rigid stalactites laced with dusty cobwebs. A path follows the stream uphill, through pine woods where the smell of resin fills the air; then over stepping-stones to a small chapel. Here and there, there are old, mossy walls sunk deep in the earth and, on a cultivated terrace where pears and apples grow, the ruins under ivy of a cottage.

After the arid landscape of the islands to the south, Agathonisi, Arki, Patmos, Lipsi, Leros, Kalimnos, the green upon green of Samos is astounding. Early this morning, at the Ireon, two workmen were cutting the green undergrowth, reeds and grasses. 'If we left it for a month, it would cover the ruins.' The summer here is as dry as elsewhere, but they said that the excavations lowered the level of the land and it is now close to underground water. The paths between the stone outlines of the ancient temples and city are grassy, mown short. Tracts of impenetrable reed crowd around the perimeter. Reed and sedge warblers sing in the thickets, swallows skim overhead. A single and colossal pillar, its sections out of true but still firm, stands in relief against the backdrop of blue pine-wooded mountains. The cape by the Ireon is one of the proposed seal reserves. A fisherman, preparing nets in Pythagorion harbour, has heard nothing of this.

'Anyone who says he loves the seals,' he says, alluding to the government campaign poster, 'is a liar'. He points at a coil of pale lemon-coloured nets. 'All in shreds,' he said. 'The seals tear them to bits for the fish. I've heard there are a couple of islands where the fishermen do get compensation, but that doesn't happen here. Anyway, how can one prove that it was the seals that destroyed the nets? It's impossible.' So the fishermen take guns with them. On summer nights, when the seals are more likely to be seen, they shoot them. 'It's our livelihood, fishing. What can we do?'

On the western headland of the harbour stand the ruins of a fortress, beseiged by the Turks in 1824. A church built within its walls proclaims over its entrance 'Christ saved Samos on 6 August 1824'. The sun sinks into dark clouds and lights for a moment the brooding shape of a mountain in Turkey across the narrow straits to the east. A three-masted schooner slides quietly into view and frames itself briefly in the jagged outline of an embrasure in the ruined walls which now enclose a cemetery. Behind small glass windows set into grey and white marble headstones, wicks burn in dishes of oil. There is a sudden violent roar and a giant dark shape thunders low overhead, rattling the panes of glass in the headstones. It is a jet, taking the tail-end of the season's visitors home to Switzerland.

Margrit and Werner feel it is time to reach the Turkish harbour where they will

Two spring-flowering bulbs of Asia Minor that grow on Samos, though rarely side by side, are the yellow hyacinth, Muscari macrocarpum, *and the sweetly scented* Hyacinthus orientalis. *Also from Asia Minor is the false Apollo butterfly.*

spend the winter. Their yacht, which Werner built himself, lies in a line of ten others, all waiting their moment to cross the Samos straits from Pythagorion to Kusadasi in Turkey. Werner is heartily sick of hearing the words 'north winds' on the shipping forecast. The *meltemi*, which the fishermen assured him would stop at the end of August, has continued all September and well into October. Even the long-awaited Little Summer of St Demetrios was so little this year that it was hardly worth having. They describe a time earlier in the year when a storm caught them south of Ikaria, where the barricade of high mountains against the north sends the wind in powerful down-draughts to whip the sea below in every direction. Werner says it was like spending ten hours in a cooking pot, when eventually they anchored in the Gulf of Marathokambos.

Today, seen from the village of Platanos, the Gulf gleams silver and placid in the afternoon sun. To the west, wooded hills rise and recede in sage-green misty shapes against the light. Stacked up the hillsides, and contrasting in their neat geometric patterns with the jumble of trees, vineyards are defined with neatly maintained stone walls. To the south and east large areas of pine trees have been burnt, not just

The Imvrassos is the largest river of Samos. The myth that the goddess Hera was born on its banks led to the creation of a sanctuary nearby. The Ireon dates from prehistoric times, its altars and temples constantly rebuilt. Today black-headed buntings, one male and two female, peck for seeds on the Sacred Road (7th century BC) which linked the ancient town of Samos with the sanctuary.

Lesvos is a large, well-wooded island and so provides a good habitat for wildlife. There are many foxes in the extensive, undisturbed stretches of pine forest.

Twenty million years ago a forest on Lesvos was turned to stone as a result of volcanic activity. Some stumps remain – stone pines with ochre bark and age-rings clear in colourful cross-section.

this year but every year recently. The trees, blackened and skeletal, tumble and lean revealing the rocky barren earth beneath. No one can understand what the perpetrators hope to achieve.

We are looking for sternbergia. But apart from mallow and fleabane and cyclamen nodding against the trunks of olives, there are no flowers. 'When will it rain?' asks a woman walking up a ravine behind the seaside village of Kokkari. She has planted a few pomegranates this year in her smallholding high in the hills, and walks up to water them every week or so. The steep valley is thick in trees – poplar, plane, wild cherry, walnut, chestnut, cypress, olive, carob, juniper. In a little chapel, frescoes reflect this abundance of nature. The ceiling dome is painted not with the heads and figures of saints, but with a loosely curving pattern of grasses, like weed under the sea. There are bouquets of flowers and zigzags in ochre, green, purple. Arches are painted with the same colours but in an abstract watery pattern threaded on to the stone as though with pen and indian ink.

But we find no sternbergia until, winding down the road into the main harbour town of Samos, Werner shouts 'Yellow flowers!' Just above the cement of a hairpin bend, a group of glistening sternbergia gleam from the rocky earth.

Lesvos

In the olive groves of Lesvos, sternbergia are thick on the ground, splashes of gold against the dry earth. Everyone is waiting for rain here too. The olives, for which the island is famous, need early autumn rain to swell on the trees. Without it, they fall to the ground, small and dry.

The walls of the town of Molivos look as though they hold all the rain that ever was. The houses are built of a dark grey-purple stone; shutters, doors and windows are painted in sombre colours, bruised purple, dark ochre, a lightless green. The sky is overcast, the day is leaden, and in the castle above the town a wind blows litter beneath benches pushed out of line by a long-departed audience of the distant summer's entertainment.

Lesvos, the third largest Greek island after Crete and Evvia, is often called by the name of its main harbour – Mitilini. As on Chios, the harbour town is reminiscent of Piraeus. Waterfront cafés are redolent of the past: on tall walls, washed eau de nil or lime blue, there is a line like a tidemark of coathooks, mirrors and curling calendars that refer to long-past dates and years. Men sit at tables on rush-seated chairs, talking and gesticulating under a haze of cigarette smoke. The ceilings are such a distance above, and the street windows so large and lit from within by strip lights, that the men appear to be some form of life living at the bottom of a fish tank. Even in the early morning, the cafés are full. The favourite food for breakfast is *patsa*. In a street behind the waterfront, in a small café called The Nest, two bowls are set before us. *Patsa* is delicious. It is entrail soup.

A fox lies on the pavement outside a butcher's shop, blood trickling from its nose. The pine woods that cover so much of the south-eastern part of the island provide shelter for fox, martens and rabbits. In the high chestnut woods above Ayiassos, a red squirrel bounds across a path. Colchicum flowers among pines, with unusually long petals and a tall triangular stem. A black and white woodpecker turns its bright red head in enquiry from an apple tree. Further west, the landscape becomes barren and rocky. In cracks between hills, there are lines of clogged greenery. In a stream lined with poplar, willows and oleanders, terrapins lie in the clear shallows looking like mottled blackish-brown stones.

If the island holds so much that is beautiful and interesting today, how much more must it have offered in the past. Little wonder that this was the background to the childhood of Theophrastus and of Sappho, and their inspiration. Would Sappho in the 6th century BC have written such poetry had she grown up elsewhere? And would Theophrastus have written 15 books on plants? Not far from Eressos, where both were born, the Petrified Forest is marked on the map. In their day it would have covered a wide area, a remarkable sight. Today, despite the map, it is almost impossible to find. At the end of a track that is more like a quarry, signs give information on the forest; how it was formed 20,000,000 years ago by volcanic activity, how the trees under lava became firestone, how tall the highest tree is (6.05 metres) and how round the thickest (8.3 metres). *Do not destroy or remove*, shout notices on every side. But one looks around in vain, seeing only lichen-covered rocks. Surely the forest hasn't been *stolen*? But this is exactly what has happened. Over the years, people have chipped away at the stone trees, and now only a few stumps remain. They look tree-like: pines with ochre bark enclosing rings of salmon pink, white, rose and crimson. There is just enough left to provoke wonder, admiration, and regret at man's cupidity.

In the shallow water of an inland stream a young terrapin stretches up its head to breathe while an adult basks on a rock in the sun. The terrapin has a more flattened shell than the tortoise and lives in or near water, feeding on aquatic animals and carrion. There are two species of terrapin in Greece, the stripe-necked and the European pond. The stripe-necked shown here gives off a repellent smell if disturbed.

A BEGINNING AND AN ENDING

That was the last of our recent Greek journeys which started in the spring of 1983 in Athens and Crete and finished on Lesvos in 1985. As we waited for a plane back to Athens, a fox ran across the runway, the sky grew dark and low and the first autumn rain started to fall like a curtain at the end of a play. At once the smell of hillside herbs filled the air. Now notebooks, which also smell faintly of herbs, sit in the drawer of a desk in Devon while their jumbled contents begin their life beside Peter's paintings in a book.

In Athens the official responsible for wildlife at the Ministry of Agriculture said, 'Regarding conservation, we are at zero'. Programmes must be based on knowledge and as yet there has been little research. 'We can't make plans for preservation until we know what we have to preserve.' There are not the funds for research, nor for public education, nor for compensation to fishermen and farmers, nor for adequate policing on sea and land. There are only 300 guards but 300,000 licensed hunters. The implementation of hunting controls is not a vote-winner.

Outside the streets were filled with demonstrators. The drachma had suffered a sudden and severe devaluation. Now we read of a further fall and more unrest. The news, like all bad news during the time we have known Greece, fills us with concern. It is as though a close relation were suffering. It is most unlikely that the government and the people will start working to preserve the natural world while richer nations destroy it on a larger scale. Yet preserve it we must, not just in Greece but everywhere, or we cannot survive ourselves. We are all part of a circle, as even the two lads on Leros realized. Wildlife knows no boundaries; neither should we when we work to make all nations aware of the natural world and our dependence on it.

Devon, 1986

Colchicum and autumn cyclamen flowering in late October on the steep, wooded slopes above the village of Ayiassos on Lesvos.

ACKNOWLEDGEMENTS

Our thanks to all the people who talked with us, helped us and gave us information on the way. The names of some of them appear in the book but we would like to send special thanks to Byron Antipas and Peter Broussalis of the Hellenic Society for the Protection of Nature;* John Koutsis; Nikos Saxonis; Martin Young; Anthony Huxley and William Taylor for permission to quote from their *Flowers of Greece*; and the authors of all the other books we have travelled with, learnt from, and now recommend in the list below.

We are most grateful to Gerald Durrell for giving our book the accolade of a foreword.

Most of all we would like to thank the people who make travelling in Greece such a pleasure – the Greeks themselves, the custodians of the land and its wildlife.

* For those who would like to support the work of HSPN, the address is 24 Nikis Street, 105 57 Athens, Greece.

BIBLIOGRAPHY

Collins Bird Guide, S. Keith & J. Gooders (Collins, 1980).

Flight Identification of European Raptors, R.P. Porter, I. Willis, S. Christensen and B.P. Nielsen (T. & A.D. Poyser, 1981).

Seabirds, P. Harrison (Croom Helm, 1983).

The Breeding Birds of Europe, vols. 1 and 2, M. Pforr and A. Limbrunner (Croom Helm, 1982).

The Country Life Guide to Birds of Britain and Europe, B. Bruun (Country Life, 1978).

Let's Look at North East Greece, M. Shepherd (Ornitholidays Guides, 1983).

Flowers of Greece and the Aegean, A. Huxley and W. Taylor (Chatto & Windus, 1984).

Flowers of Europe: a Field Guide, O. Polunin (Oxford University Press, 1969).

Flowers of the Mediterranean, O. Polunin and A. Huxley (Chatto & Windus, 1978).

Wild Orchids of Britain and Europe, P. and J. Davies and A. Huxley (Chatto & Windus, 1983).

Greek Flora, H. Bauman, Greek translation by P. Broussalis (HSPN, Athens, 1984).

A Field Guide to the Butterflies of Britain and Europe, L.G. Higgins and N.D. Riley (Collins, 1970).

A Field Guide to the Mammals of Britain and Europe, F.H. van den Brink (Collins, 1967).

A Field Guide to the Reptiles and Amphibians of Britain and Europe, E.N. Arnold and J.A. Burton (Collins, 1980).

Amphibians of Europe, D. Ballasina (David & Charles, 1984).

Guide to the Flora and Fauna of the Mediterranean Sea, A.C. Campbell (Hamlyn, 1982).

Fishes of the Sea, J. and G. Lythgoe (Blandford, 1971).

Blue Guide: Greece, S. Rossiter (Ernest Benn, 1981).

Corfu and the other Ionian Islands, M. Young (Jonathan Cape, 1981).

Nature (bulletins of HSPN, Athens).

The Mountains of Greece, G. Sfikas (Efstathiadis, Athens, 1978).

INDEX